Books by Victoria Y. Pellegrino

*The Book of Hope: How Women Can
Overcome Depression*
Coauthored by Helen De Rosis, M.D.

Living and Loving After Divorce
Coauthored by Catherine Napolitane

The
Other Side
of
Thirty

The Other Side of Thirty

Victoria Y. Pellegrino

Rawson, Wade Publishers, Inc. • New York

Library of Congress Cataloging in Publication Data

Pellegrino, Victoria Y
    The other side of thirty.

    Includes bibliographies and index.
    1. Middle aged women—United States.   2. Middle
aged women—United States—Psychology.   3. Middle
aged women—Employment—United States.   4. Divorce
—United States.   I. Title.
HQ799.97.U5P44   305.2′4   78–64861
ISBN 0–89256–073–8

Published simultaneously in Canada by McClelland
and Stewart, Ltd.
Manufactured in the United States of America
Composition by American–Stratford Graphic Services
    Brattleboro, Vermont
Printed and bound by Fairfield Graphics,
    Fairfield, Pennsylvania

Designed by Gene Siegel
First Edition

Some of the names used in this book are real names,
used with permission. The rest are pseudonyms, used to
disguise the identities of the women quoted in this book
and to protect their privacy.

Dedicated to my family,
     my mother and father, Steve and Elsie Yurasits; my
     sisters, Mehri and Veronica; and my brothers, Steve,
     Michael, and Peter

Acknowledgments

This book is the result of the help of many wonderful people.

The idea came from Sandi Gelles-Cole, a young editor who wanted to know what it was going to be like to be on the other side of thirty. The title was her husband Dennis' idea.

When Sandi left Rawson, Wade for Dell, a fine editor, Sharon Morgan, took over the project. She devoted many long hours to working on the study, and her good humor and intelligence never failed. Without her, the final manuscript would never have been completed.

I also want to express my deep appreciation to Eleanor and Kennett Rawson who believed in the book enough to wait the three years until the final study was completed, even though we had originally hoped to finish in a one-year time frame.

Thanks next must go to all the women who participated so generously in the study, the women who answered the questionnaires without asking for anything in return, except that the truth be told about the conflict women were facing in this time of profound social upheaval. Many of the questionnaires requested anonymity, and I have tried to protect these women as much as I possibly could.

Gratitude must also be expressed to the organizations that helped distribute the questionnaires: The Young Women's Christian Association; the National Organization for Women; Federally Employed Women, and the League of Women Voters. Amanda Vaill, an editor at The Viking Press, distributed questionnaires to members of the Junior League.

Many of the newspapers that reach out to women were also helpful to us in announcing the research study and directing correspondents where to write in. We found these newspapers through a wonderful book called *Media Report to Women/Index/Directory*, published by the Women's Institute for Freedom of the Press, in Washington, D.C.

I also want to thank Larry Ratzkin who did the cover design. I love it and think he did a superb, inspired job.

Also, I want to thank, in advance, Carolyn Anthony and Gwenn Mayers who will help publicize the book so that it reaches the widest possible audience. I also want to thank Elsie DeMarzi for being so cheerful and comforting every time I called on the telephone.

Appreciation to Judy McCusker for her nice typing job.

Thanks also must go to all my women friends who were so encouraging while the book was in progress: Susan Edmiston, Judith Gerberg, Elizabeth Yeary, Margalo Ashley-Bennett, Lila Swell, Christine Fraser, Luba Zimmerman, Ann Glazier, Dian Terry, Chris Filner, Mitzi Haggard, Shelley Clayman, Cile Lord, Susan Ibraham, Linda Priebe, Janet Niles, Mary Ellen Banashek. Thanks also to Eileen Cooper who aided us in running a workshop on women in their thirties at the Eastern Women's Center.

I also want to express my appreciation to the First Women's Bank of New York and the Westchester Women's

Federal Credit Union for financial support in continuing the study.

Thanks also to editor Alan Ebert, author of *The Homosexuals,* for professional generosity and expertise and to Shirley Radl, author of *Mother's Day Is Over.*

Last, thanks to Charlotte and Andy Jacobsen for their solicitousness during our stay in Phoenica, New York.

Particular acknowledgment is due Michelle Gale, who developed the interview protocols and independently conducted a large number of interviews. In addition, her theoretical insights and personal support have been invaluable. As the writer, of course, final decisions were mine and therefore final responsibility is, too.

~~~~~~

Publisher's Note

Shortly after completing this book, Victoria Pellegrino died unexpectedly. As we mourn her untimely death, we are proud to be able to publish this book, to which she devoted the last three years of her life and of which she would have been very proud.

Contents

The
Other Side
of
Thirty

Prologue

On my thirtieth birthday, after nine years of marriage, my first husband and I separated.

I was the one who left. I packed a few belongings into a wig box and settled in at my friend Mitzi's house, before looking for a place of my own. We both cried as we blew out the candles on my birthday cake. I was indeed blowing out the past and starting over.

That I finally made the decision to leave on that particular day was not a coincidence.

Like many women of my generation, I had married when I was twenty-one. I'd never had the chance to live alone, to find out what I wanted, to test my ability to be independent. My life had settled into a dull, predictable routine, and as I neared thirty, I began to wonder, "Is this all there is?" I was getting older, frightened that time was running out, and I felt desperate to answer this question.

At about the same time, I joined a consciousness-raising group and became increasingly involved in the women's movement. The experience changed my life. What a relief to discover that other women felt as I did. As we shared our stories and our anger, I began to reexamine the assumptions and expectations that I had, until then, taken for granted. Why did I have to lead the sort of life my mother did? What would it be like to strike out on my own, to live without a man?

Freedom. The idea was intoxicating . . . compelling. I was, after all, a member of a generation of women caught up in the fight for women's rights, a battle that transformed our minds, our hearts. New choices enticed me, new possibilities irrevocably shaped the nature of my dreams. For the first time, I began to feel that I had the right to please myself —not my mother, not my husband, not my bosses, but me.

I was no longer the same girl who had celebrated, with teased hair, her sweet-sixteen party, worrying if boys would like her. Nor the white-gloved woman in her college dorm, so eager to please and do what was expected. Nor the married woman of twenty-nine, already feeling that she was "over the hill."

I began to wonder if other women in their thirties were facing similar crises and conflicts. Then, by a peculiar quirk of fate, a twenty-eight-year-old editor called me to say that she was frightened about turning thirty and wanted to know what it was going to be like. Could I possibly be the writer who could tell her?

I immediately said yes to this wonderful proposal. Here was a way to understand and describe what the thirties mean to today's generation of women. I wanted to find out what other women were facing, how they were coping, how they felt about their lives. I wanted to know what was working and what wasn't. And what I found in my search, after talking to hundreds of women and listening to their stories, was that new and wonderful beginnings were possible on the other side of thirty.

As a starting point, my twenty-three-year-old research

associate and I devised an eight-page questionnaire that we distributed with the help of the League of Women Voters, the Junior League, the National Organization for Women, Federally Employed Women, the Young Women's Christian Association, and other women's organizations to women in their thirties across America. (See Appendix.)

The response to the questionnaire was quite amazing. Many women wrote in long essays about their lives, which went far beyond what I had asked for. Some women said they felt the questionnaire helped them understand their own lives better. Some said they had never been given a chance to talk about their own experiences and that they were grateful for the opportunity to do so.

We ended up with a wide-ranging sample of little more than one thousand women. I heard from homemakers, career women, Black, Chicano, and American Indian women, Catholics, Jews, Baptists and Unitarians. I heard from university professors as well as secretaries.

One fact that was immediately clear was that there was no "typical" woman in her thirties, as the television commercials would have us believe. I heard from intellectual homemakers, single-mother farmers, lesbian marketing directors, Black feminists, and executives who made over thirty-five thousand dollars a year.

I heard from women who were in despair over the mess their lives were in, as well as from women who declared that they were having the best time of their lives, and that this was, indeed, the best of times for women.

I also spent two years traveling across the country, talking to women and thinking about our problems. How astonishing it was to hear women in New Orleans, Santa Monica, Nashville, and Kansas City, confiding the same conflicts, having the same problems.

This report, then, is a distillation of the common experiences shared by this unique generation—a generation that is both victim and vanguard of social change. It will explore some of the vital questions facing women in their thirties today: What social and economic barriers do women still face? What support systems do they need to structure into their lives? What does independence feel like to the woman who lives alone? How do single women cope with loneliness? What do married women think about the institution of marriage? Why are so many over-thirty women divorcing? What have women gained or lost in divorce rights? What happens to the woman who does not make new choices for herself? How are women handling their new sexual freedom?

This book attempts to answer some of these questions and to speak to the challenges that face our entire generation of women as we move into the crucial years of the 1980s.

1

The Crucial Decade

A woman crosses the brook over thirty. She may leap over it with great gusto, assured that life can only become more wonderful. Or she can cross it with confusion and trepidation. We were raised, after all, to believe that over thirty was over the hill.

It is rather disconcerting, therefore, for a woman to find that the years over thirty are not at all what she expected.

According to Mildred Newman and Bernard Berkowitz, therapists and coauthors of *How to Be Your Own Best Friend,* the years from thirty to forty are the "crucial and most difficult" developmental decade in a woman's life. During these years a woman must resolve major identity questions, and the choices and decisions she makes will profoundly influence every aspect of her future.

Is This All There Is?

The woman over thirty starts singing a tune called, is this all there is? She may have believed, when she was

7

twenty-one, that marriage and motherhood would be the fulfillment of all her dreams. Now that she's not a starry-eyed kid anymore, she knows better. And she wonders, is this all there is?

The over-thirty married woman looks across the break-fast table at her husband and thinks, he's dull in bed. He doesn't bring me roses anymore, or even talk to me very much. As she fantasizes about an extramarital affair or con-templates divorce, she asks herself, is this all there is?

The single woman who's never had a baby becomes a little desperate as the years pass. God, she's not getting any younger! She worries about losing her looks and longs for the security of marriage. Alone in a studio apartment, she asks herself, is this all there is?

The working woman begins to panic, struggling in the fist of the Deadline Decade. She starts to dream bigger dreams than the ones she's always had. She feels enormous pressure to make new, serious choices about where she is going and how she is going to get there. As she sits stuck in a dead-end job, dreaming of success, she asks herself, with a lump in her throat, is this all there is?

Turning thirty is a critical watershed in our lives be-cause we're suddenly forced to confront the fact that we're no longer terrific kids with potential. Many of the women I heard from reported that they spent their twenties in what one termed, "a holding pattern," waiting for the right man, the right job—waiting, in fact, for their real lives to begin.

But if our youthful dreams haven't materialized or proved as satisfying as we had hoped by the time we reach that thirtieth birthday, we have to face the uncomfortable fact that almost one-third of our life is over—and what do we have to show for it? We may begin to feel that we've done everything wrong, that we should have taken ourselves more seriously in our twenties.

Over and over, women in their thirties used words like "anxious," "frustrated," "confused," and "depressed" to describe their lives. And more than once during my interviews women turned to me anxiously and asked, "How am I doing in relation to other women?"

This sense of confronting a frightening deadline is precipitated, in part, by what I've come to call age stress. Because we've been taught that the years between seventeen and twenty-nine are the best years of a woman's life, we've come to dread aging with a morbid fear that sometimes seems as intense as our fear of death itself. For those are the years when our beauty and youthful charm—traditionally, our two major assets—are at their peak, when we could expect to settle into our predestined role in life—marriage and motherhood. "I was raised," said one woman, "to see thirty as the beginning of the decline of attractiveness in women. I think thirty for a woman is like forty-five for a man. It's a woman's deadline."

If we lived in a culture that celebrated and admired female maturity, we would not experience such panic as we crosssed to the other side of thirty. However, up until very recently, our society was one of the most relentlessly youth-oriented in the world. Young women were idolized, worshiped, envied, and adored. The majority of models—who define our standards of beauty—were all in their late teens or early twenties. Airline stewardesses, for example, used to be forcibly retired at age thirty-five, before they fought for the right to remain on their jobs. As a result of shifting demographic patterns and the impact of feminism, this obsession with youth is slowly diminishing. Yet the legacy lingers on. To this day *Penthouse* magazine retires its pin-ups around the age of thirty.

As our charms supposedly decrease with age, a man's charms increase. What the over-thirty man may have lost in the way of thick hair and muscle tone, he has gained in power, status, and money. He can date a twenty-one-year-old woman and expect to be envied and admired. However, even though this is slowly changing, the reaction to a forty-five-year-old woman dating a twenty-one-year-old man is still one of shocked disbelief. Why would a man prefer a thirty-nine-year-old woman to a twenty-one-year-old girl?

Thus, turning thirty can precipitate a psychological crisis because we have so few positive images to draw on.

From the responses to our questionnaire, we heard a litany. Just listen.

My thirtieth birthday was the craziest day of my life. I saw my life pass and everything that I was. And I was nothing. I had not accomplished anything. My marriage was terrible. I started seeing gray hairs and wrinkles I hadn't seen the day before.

I spent the day walking the streets, trying to find myself. I was confused about religion. I didn't want to be a Jew anymore, so I went to St. Patrick's Cathedral, a Catholic Church. That wasn't the answer either.

A thirty-three-year-old
homemaker

Turning thirty was traumatic. I cried and cried. I was scared and kept wondering, where am I?

A thirty-six-year-old divorcée
with a fifteen-year-old son

A week before I was going to be thirty-five, I found myself very depressed. I couldn't get out of bed to get to the office. I thought, if anyone gives me wrinkle cream for my birthday, I'll scream.

*I always felt that I was preparing to live. And
there I was in the middle of my life! I felt tremendous pressure to decide whether to buy a home, have
a child, change my career.*

> A thirty-five-year-old director
> of publications for a women's
> health center

Moreover, we face a special agony in the fourth decade
of our lives—the beginning of the end of our reproductive
function, the very essence of our identity as females. For the
childless woman, the decision whether or not to have a child
becomes an overwhelming pressure. And even for the
woman who's had a number of children, there is a poignant
feeling of sadness associated with the knowledge that a crucial part of her life—bearing and nurturing babies—is slowly
coming to an end.

These biological pressures translate into a feeling that
time is running out. According to Judith M. Bardwick, a
psychologist and author of *The Psychology of Women,*
women in their thirties "feel it imperative to gratify their
needs now—because otherwise they may never do it." But
while this pressure tugs at us and encourages us to dream
new dreams, we're hampered by an equally strong feeling
that it's already too late, that new beginnings are not possible on the other side of thirty.

The fact is, women are not used to looking at their
lives as a developmental process. We were brought up to
believe that all our choices would be made *before* age thirty;
that the rest of our lives would simply be a calm, predictable
extension of those decisions. We have inherited from our
mothers a condition known as tunnel vision—an inability
to recognize that choices and options for growth are still
possible.

A Female Legacy: Our Mothers' Lives

If we understand our mothers' lives, we can better understand our own.

Their lives were, for the most part, severely restricted by traditional values and rigid role definitions that were embraced by the media and other shapers of our culture with a fervor bordering on mystical intensity. Based on centuries of conditioning that held that women were the physical and mental inferiors of men, our mothers learned that they could seek no higher goal in life than marriage and motherhood. The paragon of American womanhood, plastered over the pages of every popular women's magazine in the 1950s was the stay-at-home wife, doing her part to fulfill the American dream by bearing and raising babies, caring for that cherished home in the suburbs, and supporting her upwardly mobile husband. While husband and children went off into the world, she kept the home fires burning, creating a comfortable haven to which they could return and forget the rigors of their day. Marriage and family togetherness were sacrosanct; divorce unthinkable, except in the most extreme cases.

Consequently, the pattern of their lives *was* already set by the time they were in their thirties. And the rest of their lives *were* a predictable—if not calm—extension of the decisions they'd made in their twenties. Most had married young (what else was there to do?) and expected to remain married. By the time they turned thirty they were busy raising children and caring for home and husband. If they had energy, ambition, or curiosity extending beyond the home, they threw themselves into volunteer work. Few women thought in terms of a career, of the satisfactions men traditionally expect from a job. Indeed, most pitied the small minority of unmarried and/or childless women who struggled to make it in a man's world. Such women were said to be neurotic, unable to accept their femininity, consumed by penis envy.

Consider, for example, what our mothers were reading in the women's magazines during the 1950s. The popular—and still enduring—monthly feature in *The Ladies' Home Journal*, "Can This Marriage Be Saved?" offered this case history in 1950. Kyra, married at nineteen and pregnant shortly thereafter, decides to divorce her husband, get a job, and raise her child alone after she discovers that he's been gambling heavily.

However, at a marriage counseling session, Kyra learns that their difficulties are her fault. Her husband gambles because she is too dominating. According to the counselor, Kyra has deprived him of the "gaiety, fun, and freedom" he had experienced in the Army. She is "a clever, softspoken modern version of the critical, domineering mother." The counselor's solution? Kyra must change her attitude and stop asking her husband to help her dry dishes and wash diapers.

In another case history in this same series, published in 1957, the wife, an amateur pilot, is delighted to give her husband the divorce he's asked for. But their marriage counselor encourages them to work out their problems, offering the following analysis: "Mistrustful of her own femininity . . . she has gone into active competition with him, and thus lowered his slender store of self-confidence and made him miserable." To restore balance in their relationship, she is advised to quit her flying lessons and learn to enjoy cooking, cleaning, and caring for her husband. "Few husbands," we are solemnly told, "are encouraged by being outdone by their wives."

Our mothers' total dependence on men—both economically and emotionally—stemmed from this discouragement of an active female voice. Deprived of healthy self-expression, a woman was forced to seek identity and self-esteem by pleasing and living through a man. Women gave themselves up in the name of love and family because they had little choice.

> *My mother married at eighteen, had two children, worked full-time, helped support her parents, and only did the oil painting she loved on her vacations. Sacrificing her needs for her family, she remained a dilettante all her life.*
>
> A thirty-three-year-old artist

> *My mother died three years ago, but I'm sure that when she was still alive in the early seventies, she thought I had lost my mind. She was a traditional housewife who never contradicted her husband, even when he was dead wrong. She went through a great deal of trauma when I divorced, and later lived with a man.*
>
> A thirty-four-year-old musician

> *My mother wouldn't even balance a checkbook.*
>
> A thirty-seven-year-old executive officer for an insurance company

Because we are our mothers' daughters, most of us grew up expecting to follow the same pattern, to have settled, stable lives in our thirties. Indeed, the majority of women in this study duplicated these traditional expectations.

> *I was raised with the expectation to marry, have children, and live happily ever after. I was shocked when I was divorced.*
>
> A thirty-nine-year-old mother

Like all young girls in the 1950s, I thought life was a process that involved finishing school, meeting and marrying Prince Charming, and living happily ever after. All our dreams seemed to end around age twenty-five.

A thirty-two-year-old silver-
smith

My expectations as a young girl were unbelievably traditional. I remember a ninth-grade career note-book with three alternatives. Teacher. Nurse. Stewardess. I decided to teach, but only until I married and raised a family like my mother. I would have died at the thought of ending up a spinster.

A thirty-six-year-old editor

Like our mothers, we were not encouraged to have careers or dreams that went beyond marriage and mother-hood. While our brothers came and went with relative free-dom, we learned how to be "good girls"—polite, submissive, self-effacing, and accommodating to the men in our lives. The truly feminine woman subordinated her own goals and desires for those whom she loved—her parents, her boy-friends, her husband, her children. Those were the "good girl" rules, as the following story eloquently attests:

> *I went to two universities, Penn State and Ohio Wesleyan, and can't think of a single female who had the individuality to break out of the stereotypical feminine role. All of us were getting engaged by our senior year.*
>
> *In the days before the pill, the freedom of hav-ing guilt-free sex was probably the single best reason to get married. I would have died before going to a*

doctor to be fitted for a diaphragm without an engagement ring.

I married my husband when I graduated and taught elementary school while he got his MBA at Wharton. Then I had a baby. It never occurred to me that I had alternatives. I never considered having a career of my own, or postponing marriage until I went to graduate school myself.

My college roommate and best friend made Phi Beta Kappa in her junior year. At graduation, she won two full scholarships to study for her doctorate. Her first semester, she fell in love with a brilliant young professor, quit school, got married, and had babies.

The only other woman I know who went on for further education married an engineer who convinced her to quit working, become a gourmet cook and partygiver, and be ready to travel with him at the drop of a hat.

A thirty-eight-year-old medical
secretary with two children

How confusing, therefore, to discover that these rules are suddenly obsolete, that there are *still* so many question marks in our over-thirty lives.

As I talked to women for this book—as they wrote to me or confided their pain in long conversations that stretched far into the evening—it became patently clear that very few women of my generation have their lives wrapped up in a neat little package by age thirty, thirty-five, or even forty. If we are failures, we are all failures together.

Indeed, far from being a settled decade, the thirties today are years in which women experience dramatic and unexpected changes. This is not an indication of failure but a *normal developmental pattern for the historic times in which we live.* For we are a generation in transition between a traditional past and an unexplored future; the first generation to have come to maturity during the upheaval caused by the rise of feminism, the sexual revolution, the activist legacy of the sixties, and the liberating as well as bewildering human potential movement of the seventies.

What I've discovered—the very thesis of this book—is that the over-thirty woman is undergoing a profound psychological and sociological transition as she struggles to define herself not according to the traditional roles of masculine and feminine but in more fully human ways. Current statistics bear this out. Today, the years between thirty and forty are breakthrough years for many women, years of new beginnings and new choices that are both frightening and exhilarating.

- The age of the average divorcée is thirty-six.
- Women in their thirties are returning to school in huge numbers.
- Over 25 percent of women have their first extramarital affair in their thirties.
- A significant number have their first orgasms and/or their first homosexual affair.
- Thirty-five is the average age of the runaway wife.
- Thirty-six is the average age for a second marriage.
- The greatest number of adoptions by single women take place when they're between the ages of thirty-five and thirty-nine.
- Motherhood after thirty is being chosen by more and more women.
- Women make major career breakthroughs between ages thirty and forty.

These statistics graphically illustrate that today's woman is living in an age of choices, what one thirty-seven-year-old respondent called the age of ambivalence.

As Ann Lieberman, an assistant professor in the Curriculum Teaching Department at Columbia University, says, "Women in their thirties today have to deal with choices that women in their forties and fifties did not have to deal with at that age. Although the possibilities might have been there, they weren't really acceptable social alternatives. There really is a choice for women today, a choice to be single, a choice to follow a career rather than to be a mother, a choice to do both.

"Options make it difficult because choice is hard. There's a tremendous amount of struggle around these questions: Should I marry? Should I work? Should I have children? Should I return to school? Should I divorce? Should I have an affair?

"I think these choices are giving women in their thirties today fits."

What I found confirms Lieberman's thesis. For the voices I heard throughout my research were not the same voices Betty Friedan listened to when she wrote her seminal book *The Feminine Mystique* and exploded the myth that American women were happy housewives, content to remain within the confines of hearth and home. In our study, there was a dinosaur here and there, but even the trapped housewife, the bored, resigned, or scared woman was changing, sometimes even in spite of herself!

And this relates directly to what has happened to us historically. For, as Arlene Skolnick, research psychologist at the Institute of Human Development at the University of California at Berkeley, says, "Women in their thirties are really the leading edge of a new generation of people who have gone through the changes of the sixties and come out the other side. They are the pioneers in a new life-style. They are moving ahead without very many role models to guide them."

Pioneers in a new life-style. Think about that. For if you keep in mind that we are pioneers—that as a generation we are not only historic but heroic—you will come to see why our lives often seem so chaotic, so puzzling, so painful. Why the question of identity is so unsettling. For all this change happened so fast that it's hard to assimilate. And we continue to carry our mother's values inside us. Therein lies the conflict—between the old and the new.

What we must keep in mind, therefore, is that we're living through an exciting but anxiety-producing time in which all values are in flux. Today, life has much more fluidity than it had for our mothers and grandmothers. We will move in and out of marriages, careers, relationships, with much greater frequency than traditional mores would have led us to expect. Although an issue may be dormant or satisfactorily resolved for months or years at a time, an ultimate solution may be impossible. Nothing is forever.

Our entire generation of women has been affected by the profound social revolutions of the last fifteen years, whether we participated directly or not. Yet this does not mean that we have turned, overnight, into independent "New Women." It's not that simple. A woman may yearn to be sexually free, to experience wild heights of passion, yet find herself too inhibited and unable to have orgasms. A woman may want a career but be unable to choose a direction. A woman may seek independence, yet be troubled by the pangs of loneliness that are part of the single life.

The point is that social upheaval hasn't already happened *but is now in the process of happening.* Thus, we cannot judge ourselves by unrealistic standards, whether they are the standards our mothers lived by or the new Superwoman standards. Most of us don't realize that the conflicts we experience are shared by other women. Social change, after all, is the product of thousands upon thousands of individual choices being made in fear and relative isolation. One of the purposes of this book is to help women—whether they are twenty, thirty, forty, or fifty—understand where they are today, where they have been, and where they are going.

"The rapid social changes are manifestations of a long-run social and economic evolution," states Larry Hirschorn of the University of Pennsylvania in a pamphlet called *Social Policy and the Life Cycle: A Developmental Perspective.* "The principal cause for these changes seem to me to be the result of the greater emphasis placed upon the individual, and the greater legitimacy accorded to a variety of life choices. . . .

"This is in contrast to the earlier emphasis on the nuclear family and its stability as the dominant mode. The reasons for the change in emphasis lie in the increasing education of the population, which has revealed the variety of choices open to individuals, and broadened the range of choices acceptable under evolving social norms."

The choices open to us today make it both the best and worst of times. It is confusing to be part of a transitional generation, making choices our mothers did not make at our age. Because we are pioneers, we must expect, and learn to cope with, a certain amount of anxiety, depression, and stress. However, the story doesn't end there. "Are there happy endings for women today?" one thirty-two-year-old divorcée asked me, as I was midway through this report. "Absolutely," I said. The strongest message I want to convey is that transitions can and do have positive outcomes. Life can be very difficult, but new choices can lead to incredible growth and self-discovery.

Transitions seem to take from two to five years to resolve. For example, a woman who is undergoing a divorce or changing careers may experience an incredibly difficult period of adjustment, complete with depression, fear, and inertia. Anxiety always accompanies change, since one has abandoned the past and faces an uncertain future.

However, the stress of transition is the price our generation is paying for having, for the first time in history, freedom to choose. As women make new choices, moreover, they discover the most astonishing things—strength and talent they had no idea they had when they were younger. Listen again.

I had no voice in my twenties. I found it in my thirties.

A thirty-four-year-old accountant

In my twenties I was on the outside looking at myself. Now I'm on the inside looking out.

A thirty-two-year-old singer

I see myself as possessing more power and energy in relation to other people now.

A thirty-five-year-old Chicano woman who launched a personnel career at thirty-one

I was so insecure at thirty. But today I know who I am. By forty I had changed so much it felt completely different than I'd expected it to be.

A forty-one-year-old owner of a major decorating firm

I love being thirty-six. I'm happier now than I've ever been. I feel confident of my ability to deal with other people, and with most any situation which

arises. If I'd known how great it would be to be over thirty, I never would have worried about getting older.

A single mother of two

I am a mensch and a professional. I respect myself more than I did when I was in my twenties.

A thirty-four-year-old university professor

Interestingly, this pattern of development has historical precedent. In the midst of this study, in an attempt to track down positive role models, I spent a summer in the library reading biographies of famous women. What I discovered was exciting, for all of the following women began to recognize their talent and goals only after the age of thirty. I realized that there was a story of female adult development that had yet to be told.

The Breakthrough Years

• The writer Edith Wharton suffered from a nervous collapse and depression between the years thirty-two and thirty-four. She felt her problem was an inability to make choices, exacerbated by her unhappiness in her marriage. At thirty-six she was again bedridden for depression. After that, however, she began to write, and gifted us with many magnificent books including *Ethan Frome* and *The Age of Innocence*. By the time she was in her fifties, like writers Colette and Virginia Woolf, she knew her own power and was a supremely confident woman.

• As she reached thirty, the slave Harriet Tubman faced the prospect of being sold to a Georgia slave trader. She escaped with the help of a white woman and began her underground railroad, mounting the lecture platform for the first time at age thirty-eight.

• At twenty-four, Marie Curie left for Paris to study physics. After marriage and a child, she did her first independent research study at thirty-one. Between the years thirty-two to thirty-six, which she called "the heroic period of our common existence," she and her husband discovered radium. She tells us: "Life is not easy for any of us. But what of that? We must have perseverance and, above all, confidence in ourselves. We must believe that we are gifted for something and that this thing, at whatever cost, must be attained."

• At the age of thirty, designer Coco Chanel opened her first hat shop, which was financed by Arthur Capel, whom she planned to marry. When he disappointed her, according to her biographer, she was determined to become an independent woman. Work became "her only source of satisfaction." In her thirties, she achieved financial success and bought her first villa.

• The writer Charlotte Perkins Gilman divorced at thirty-five and sent her only daughter to live with her father because she felt she could not care for her. In her diary she wrote that she felt like a "failure, a repeated, cumulative failure."

However, the next year she went abroad to attend a Labor Congress. Traveling abroad, she tells us, led to new growth in self-confidence and belief in her own talents. At thirty-seven, she wrote the best-selling *Women and Economics,* which stressed the need for women's financial independence. It was one of the most important works on women written in the nineteenth century, and it brought her instant fame.

• Anna Louise Strong was one of the most significant journalists of the twentieth century. According to her biographer, the Civil War made her conscious of a need to find meaning in her own life. After a restless period of boredom around the time she turned thirty, she went to Russia with the American Friends Service. In her late thirties, she became the Russian correspondent for the North American Newspaper Alliance and began an outstanding journalistic career.

Reading these biographies made me look differently at the pattern of women's lives. For if this study and the stories of these outstanding women prove anything, it is that the years between thirty and fifty are breakthrough years for women, years in which they come to terms with their potential and define and work toward new goals and new dreams.

When I was thirty-one, my husband left me and I had to get a job for the first time in my life to support myself and my two kids. It wasn't easy and it was very scary, but now I can look back and honestly say that it was the best thing that ever happened to me. I like the person I am today, and I smile now when younger women tell me they are frightened of turning thirty. How wonderful it can be, I want to tell them. How delicious it is to have experience, wisdom, and a greater understanding of oneself and others. The over-thirty woman can have sophistication and confidence that younger women can only long for.

A thirty-seven-year-old computer programmer

2

The Marriage Seesaw:
Disappointment and Rebirth

As early as 1960 social scientists reported that married women consistently rated lower on mental health examinations than either married men or unmarried women. More married women than men reported that they were going to have nervous breakdowns; more experienced anxiety and feelings of inadequacy. Married women as a group were more depressed, phobic, and passive than single women.

Twenty years later the picture hasn't changed very much. A majority of women in this study reported that they were disappointed with their marriages. Marital dissatisfaction is, in fact, a major theme among women in their thirties. Despite the social upheaval of the last fifteen years, the changing nature of male/female relationships, and the prevalence of divorce, many women are still the victims of unsatisfactory marriages.

I went to work to help out with money, but I expected more of a sense of responsibility from my husband. I feel shocked and disappointed that he doesn't know what needs to be done, or even seem to care.

A thirty-two-year-old executive
secretary with two children

The source of my dissatisfaction is the endless time my husband spends in front of the television. I just wasn't prepared for the hours and hours he spends incommunicado. When the TV Widow Blues hit, I tell myself I should be grateful he doesn't hang out in bars, beat me, or starve me.

A thirty-six-year-old mother of
three pursuing a master's degree
in business

I grew up believing that I would marry and live happily for the rest of my life. My marriage would be perfect. I would help my husband in his career, raise my children, wear elegant gowns in the evening while I served my husband a martini after his hard day at the office. This was the romantic version of marriage I had learned in the movies and I thought it was real. I did not expect to end up a frustrated and angry housewife.

A thirty-three-year-old mother
of three

We were raised to believe that marriage would be the fulfillment of our dreams. A knight in shining armor would rescue us from dreary solitude, and we would live happily ever after. The tragedy for many women of our generation has been the discovery that this myth simply is not true. We marry to pursue this romantic dream, whereas, in fact, much of marriage is labor, not romance. Many, many women complained bitterly about the lack of sharing, communication, and support in their marriages. Over and over again, I heard the same words of angry surprise: "I did *not expect* to end up a frustrated and angry housewife." "I *expected more* of a sense of responsibility from my husband." "I just *wasn't prepared* for the hours and hours he spends incommunicado."

Unfortunately, for many unhappy women, confronting the reality does not necessarily mean that escape or change is possible. Many feel trapped—by their "good girl" upbringing, by their emotional dependence on men, by their lack of financial resources. They believe that a bad marriage is better than no marriage at all, and they seek the same kind of security that their mothers seemed to have.

Traditionally, marriage has been based on the dual concepts of male privilege and female self-sacrifice. Marriage was not a route to personal development or growth for a woman. Her role was to put husband and children first. These were the rules our mothers lived by, and for them, as we've seen, there was very little choice. If some of them did feel resentment or bitterness, they suppressed it, knowing they would receive little support or understanding from other women or society at large. They assumed it was some flaw in their own character, an inability to accept their feminine role. And there was no question about that role; it was hammered home in every major women's magazine. In 1955, for example, in *The Ladies' Home Journal,* marriage counselor Clifford Adams told women that responsible wives do not become bored with housework or ask their husbands to help. They accept their husbands' criticisms even if they think he is being unfair, and they always serve meals on time, even if they hold outside jobs.

Growing up in the 1950s, playing with our dolls and dreaming of our weddings, how could we help but internalize these rules and make them our own?

The Good Girl Wife

Jane is a thirty-eight-year-old medical secretary with three children. She married at twenty-one because it was expected of her. "I completely sublimated my interests and my desires to my husband," she wrote. "My only contacts were my neighbors, and his friends and colleagues. Vaguely, I knew I was unhappy, but I didn't know why."

At thirty-three, when her children were old enough, she decided to return to work. She wanted a job with a future but wasn't sure where or how to start.

"I'm convinced," she said, "that the biggest problem of our generation is the men. My husband thinks I should have a better career, and yet he doesn't lift one finger to help me with the housework. He leaves me full responsibility for the children. He expects me to wait on him hand and foot and complains bitterly if the house is messy, dinner is late, or there aren't enough towels in the linen closet. His abuse has always been verbal. He is a classic male chauvinist.

"On bad days, I fantasize about telling him off and walking out. After what he has put me through I have no more sexual attraction to him. But I believe in marriage and family, we both love the children, and I have no independent means of support. I find myself thoroughly invested in a situation which is making it almost impossible for me to grow."

Jane is a classic example of the "good girl" wife as martyred victim. Although she doesn't think it's fair, she adheres to the "good girl" rules and waits on her husband hand and foot, repressing her own resentment and anger.

And she does this not only because her husband expects her to but because deep down *she herself* believes she should. This image of what a good wife should be is a direct product of the romantic myths of marriage we were brought up to believe in.

A woman named Karen wrote in to say that she, like many of her contemporaries, believed that if she was a good homemaker and mother, her marriage would be perfect. She was confused by her husband's involvement with other women, and she wondered what was wrong with her and what she could do to improve her marriage. In desperation she sought marital counseling.

She felt the marriage was improving until her husband suggested wife swapping. Like a "good wife," she complied but found it an ordeal. Her explanation: "I am a one-man woman, while he needs attention from other women and handles it badly."

Like so many women of her generation, Karen was taught that in pleasing her husband she would please herself. Although experience has dispelled this myth, she can't quite relinquish the notion that the failure of her marriage is somehow her fault. Her sense of self and her identity are too wrapped up in her role as wife. And without an independent income, she feels powerless to seek a divorce or demand that her husband adhere to their monogamous contract. Marriage has made her a victim, and she feels too old, too terrified, to begin a new life.

Another large group of women complained about being uprooted by their husbands' jobs. Their lives are continually disrupted, and while many bear it in silence, they are inwardly angry and lost.

His job moved us to Tucson, and has moved us four more times in the last eight years. I feel as if I've

*never been able to build a life of my own. We've
lived in twenty different cities.*

> A thirty-eight-year-old corpo-
> rate wife who was married
> when she was seventeen

Women pay a price for such moves, namely the relin-
quishment of financial independence and autonomous self-
development. It is almost impossible to have a career of your
own while continually moving for your husband's career.
And the responsibilities involved in resettling, making new
friends, dealing with the children's reaction to change, and
entertaining a husband's business associates are exhausting
and time-consuming.

If such marriages break up, and many do, a woman will
be among the lucky few if she receives any alimony. She certainly will not get any compensation from the corporation
she served as faithfully as her husband.

Sadly, it seems that even in these enlightened eighties,
many married women are unable to break out of subservient, often masochistic roles, despite the devastating effect
on their personal integrity. The problem is that we feel a
tremendous amount of guilt when we violate the self-
sacrificing "good girl" rules we learned in childhood. Even
today the image of the married woman as a kind of victimized Edith Bunker is all too prevalent in the media and
still firmly embedded in the minds of women themselves.
We women laughed at the antics in the Bunker household,
but did our laughter have a trace of uneasiness as we recognized in Edith's perennial role as placator and peacemaker
a part of ourselves?

But the woman who continues to sacrifice her own
needs builds up a tremendous store of anger that will find
expression—in one way or another. The price of silence can

be anything from an inability to enjoy sex or cope with the most routine aspects of daily life, to severe depression. And depression is contagious, affecting all family members and placing a great strain on all relationships.

Battered Wives

Nowhere do we see the state of marital female oppression more clearly than when we look at studies on wife beating.

Recent hearings conducted by Senator Alan Cranston (Democrat from California) on domestic violence disclosed that in California, one of our most populous states, one out of two women will be assaulted by her husband or son at some time in her life.

The hearings further disclosed:

• One-fourth of all battered women are pregnant.

• One-third of all female murder victims are killed by their husbands.

Studies also show that the rate of child abuse is 129 percent higher in families where there is also wife abuse. Eighty percent of men who batter their wives were battered children or had fathers who beat their mothers, which shows how powerful role modeling is.

The battered woman needs help badly. Thirty-seven-year-old Cathleen, a beautiful, California mother of two, told me she was a battered wife in her early twenties. "Do you know what a battered wife experiences?" she asked. "It's a terror that's so overwhelming there is no place to hide. You have to get your fear under control—especially if you have children—or you'll go out of your mind."

The first time her husband beat her, Cathleen said, she didn't believe it. After each attack, he promised it would not happen again. But it always did.

Cathleen realized she was living with a maniac, a man

who could be charming and considerate one minute and furious the next.

When his rage erupted, there was nothing but pain strung out over the bedroom walls . . . the sink . . . the living-room couch. After years of enduring beatings while trying to get help for her husband, Cathleen finally came to believe she was entitled to a divorce.

It is a commonplace myth, says Cathleen, that all battered women are passive and masochistic. Many, like Cathleen, are unable to divorce simply because of legal, social, and economic reasons. They have no incomes of their own, and they are frightened of living alone. That overwhelming fear conditioned into them—life without a man—continues to haunt them and limit their choices.

Police, moreover, are reluctant to prosecute batterers, and very few are ever thrown in jail. If a woman wants to leave, she may have nowhere to go unless she has money. There are very few shelters available for battered women, in spite of the great need for them.

Furthermore, the battered wife receives little emotional support from society. Consider, for example, the advice Norman Vincent Peale gave a battered wife in a February 1979 column in a California newspaper called *The Enterprise.*

This woman wrote in to say that her husband was having an affair with a woman ten years younger than she was but that even an affair hadn't helped his disposition. He beat her all the time. "I have been in emergency rooms more than once," she wrote. "You try to tell yourself he will quit. I need help."

Dr. Peale answered her appeal with the following: "Your husband seems to evidence an unconscious need to dominate. Stand up, but don't mention the other woman. Perhaps if you become more of a strong woman he might quit running around. Be controlled, even aloof, and keep a good home. . . ."

Nowhere in his answer does the author indicate that she is *entitled* to walk out. The "good girl" wife stays with her husband, even if he ends up killing her.

Wife beating, chauvinism, and other forms of male abuse seem to be all too common in American marriages. I was shocked when I saw the statistics and read the questionnaires from miserable over-thirty wives.

Does this mean that marriage is a doomed institution? That it's impossible for a woman to find happiness as a wife? Not at all. A large number of over-thirty wives reported that their marriages were better than ever. What characterizes these women is their willingness to break out of the "good girl" mold, to assert themselves, often at the risk of losing their husbands, and to strive for an equal partnership. The first step for most of them was the realization that they were indeed *entitled* to the same pleasures and privileges as their husbands. And with that sense of entitlement comes the self-esteem necessary to make changes.

An Alcoholic Homemaker Finds Self-Esteem

Joyce Burditt is a forty-two-year-old former alcoholic homemaker. She is the author of *The Cracker Factory,* a novelized version of her struggle to overcome alcoholism and a series of nervous breakdowns. She has three children and has recently completed her second novel, *Triplets,* which will be published by Delacorte later this year.

In her twenties, she was a drinking housewife, bored by her life and her marriage. "George came home from work, read the newspaper, ate dinner and watched television. On Saturdays, he played golf, and Sunday was his day to putter around. I resented this because it meant I didn't have a day off. On Saturdays, I did the grocery shopping, went to the drugstore and the dry cleaners.

"On Sunday, I was always saying, 'Can't we do something fun?' He'd say, 'Well we have to cut the lawn . . . or trim the hedges . . . or shoot the raccoons in the backyard'! Whatever it was that he was doing!

"I worked seven days a week. I was drinking every day. I felt hopeless. I was sick. My concentration was gone. It was a massive kind of depression that I was trying to alleviate with alcohol. Then the 'solution' became the problem."

Joyce believes that women fall into drinking not realizing that it can become a disease. "Everybody drinks when they iron. Everybody has a drink when they start dinner. You forget that you're home alone drinking. How I hated ironing! I used to hide piles of ironing behind the furnace and leave it there until the kids outgrew the clothes! People give children these clothes with ruffles and bows and shirts that have to be starched. The kids wear them for an hour, and then back you are the next day, ironing these rotten puffed sleeves all over again!"

Joyce sees the isolation of the homemaker role as one of the major reasons for her drinking. "The only person I talked to was my neighbor two doors down. She had made a deal with her husband that he would get laid every other night, and that she would consider oral sex sometime in the future. I was so lonely!"

Her salvation was joining Alcoholics Anonymous and getting a part-time job as a teacher's aide. "George started helping out—he didn't mind and I didn't give him much choice." She cooked, George washed the clothes, and she got a cleaning woman once a week.

Then she went to college for a year. "There I was, romping around on a volley ball court with seventeen-year-olds! What really drove me nuts were the eighteen-year-old philosophers who were going to save the world their parents had ruined!" She did not get a degree but took a job as a script reader with Tomorrow Entertainment. She learned about writing and wrote her first novel.

"Over the last few years, my husband's consciousness has been raised. I think a lot of us in our thirties and forties have husbands whose consciousnesses were gradually raised, not necessarily by choice. My impression is that if a woman moves into her own and her husband's awareness doesn't grow, the marriage fails. A vital, independent woman doesn't have time for a man who doesn't understand that her life is as important as his. If both people are willing, it is possible to go from a very traditional marriage to a coequal partnership in which the man has grown as much or even more than the woman. It's not easy, but it can be done.

"About two years ago, George and I were separated for six months. It was a very interesting experience, and not bad overall for our marriage. We're both glad it happened. Since I married so young, I had never lived alone, and every time we had an argument and considered breaking up, George would say, 'But you've never been on your own. You wouldn't know what to do for yourself.' And I had to agree.

"As it turned out, I loved living alone. Now George and I are together because we choose to be, not because I can't live alone and he feels guilty about sending this defenseless little woman out into the cold, hard world.

"The idea for my second book came to me during our separation. It's about thirty-five-year-old triplets, two women and a man, one of whom works for a television network. Shortly after I started the book, I had an automobile accident. For a while it looked as though I'd never walk again. I went through three operations, two of them major surgery. It took me six months to start writing again, by which time I was seriously behind schedule on the book. It's twice as long as *The Cracker Factory*, and I wrote it in half the time. I could never have done it without my family. George was wonderful. Although he's producing "Three's Company" now, he somehow managed to pick up the dry-cleaning and do my shopping and make my dinners. I didn't come out of my study once in the last four weeks, and delivered the book one month late to the day.

"I've loved every age I've been since thirty-four. There's a lot of roads to go down before you find out that you don't want to go down those roads, and most of that is over with by the time you hit forty. Maturity is really terrific. One thing I've learned to do as I zoomed through my thirties was to trust my instincts. I really love to work and I didn't know that. I grew up with everyone telling me I was lazy. I wasn't lazy. I was depressed! I just wasn't any good at being a housewife.

"I love being forty-two. I always thought that youth was overrated anyway. I began to get a sense of who I was in my early thirties, and I've got enough years left to really do some productive things. I've got nothing but material here. I'm more focused. I've realized that if you have a good relationship with your family and a few good friends, you're a very lucky person. Middle-aged doesn't mean you stop growing. It just means that a lot of the extraneous bullshit is gone. My sense of it is not that my time is getting short, but that I'm using it more wisely."

For Joyce a new beginning was possible once she broke out of the victim role and began to assert her rights for self-fulfillment and pleasure. But she was lucky, too: household help and a cooperative husband eased the transition. Work has become an important new freedom for her, bolstering her newfound self-esteem and assertiveness.

The Working Wife

Joyce's story, and other similar ones, might lead one to assume that the incidence of depression in married women is diminishing today, now that women have won the option to work outside the home. However, although it is true that many women report that their jobs have bolstered their confidence and self-esteem, many others have found that the pressures on them have simply increased. Now they're expected to be superwomen, handling three jobs effortlessly: motherhood, a career, and housework. The result, according to many of the women who wrote in, is exhaustion.

A part-time consultant at a university said that she had married when she was thirty-one; her husband was a vice-president in a medium-sized corporation. By the time she was thirty-three, she was traveling regularly for her job and had also started graduate school. "I was perpetually harassed because I had so much to do," she wrote. "There was never enough time to clean the house, do the laundry, shop for food, do the cooking, keep the closets in order, arrange a social life. I thought my husband wanted a partner, but he wanted a mother. He said the demands of my career threatened him. He needed a full-time wife, even though he said he wanted a woman who was independent and earned her own money." Finally, her husband divorced her to marry a younger, more submissive woman. "I was miserable when he left me," my correspondent wrote. "I was hoping the marriage would work right up until the end."

I was very surprised to discover that most American women were receiving so little help from their husbands. I had expected to hear that many more women were working out new, equitable arrangements in their marriages.

However, many over-thirty women still equate femininity with submissiveness. They feel guilty about asserting their rights and, without new role models, they cling to the old "good girl" rules.

Our lack of role models for new ways to relate in marriage is a serious problem. It is difficult to break old patterns in isolation. Most of us grew up watching our fathers relax with the paper, waiting for dinner to be served. Rarely, if ever, did we see our mothers sitting with their feet up while the men cooked.

"One of the hardest transitions for the married woman who desires a more equitable relationship is allowing the man to do the housework or make dinner, while she sits and relaxes, thus totally reversing traditional roles," states Dr. Norma Davies, research associate at the Mental Health Research Institute in Palo Alto, California. "Women have been told it's wrong to relax while the man is working, whereas men have never had this problem."

Most women who reported being overworked find it almost impossible to adopt a position of entitlement to service and pleasure. They feel guilty about being "selfish" and "lazy." As one Catholic woman told me, "I've been brought up with this stringent work ethic—a crazy mentality. You never relax and enjoy—ever. I'm not a tennis player; I'm a worker."

Furthermore, many over-thirty wives who immerse themselves in their role as homemakers become slaves to the "perfection syndrome." They take enormous pride in keeping their homes spotless, and once they go off to work they find it hard to let go. They are dissatisfied with the way their husbands make beds, vacuum, wash dishes, so they continue to shoulder a larger share of the burden than they can reasonably handle. Not surprisingly, most of the working wives who had split the household work load reported that they were much more relaxed about clutter and dust.

Women who are still struggling to be superwomen, unable or afraid to demand help, can take heart from this encouraging finding: Over-thirty wives who do insist on a genuine partnership report that their marriages do, in the long run, benefit enormously.

A woman married fifteen years wrote in to say: "The first ten years I was married, I was superwoman. I did everything. Then one night—it was about nine o'clock—I began to question this. I'd been going since six A.M. Up at six, breakfast for my daughter, dress and get her to school, at work all day, rush, rush to meet her after school, get her home, bathed and fed, look over homework and listen to her day, get our dinner cooked, and then clean up the kitchen. Never any time of my own.

"Meanwhile, my husband got up at eight-thirty, worked until five-thirty, came home and propped his feet up, read the newspaper and drank beer until midnight.

"On this night, the basic injustice of it all hit me and I blew up like two tons of dynamite. This was a mistake, and put him on the defensive for two years. I wish I had done it differently, but I couldn't help it. I didn't realize how much resentment had built up.

"Things have changed, however. We still aren't fifty-fifty, but sixty-five–thirty-five. And the marriage is in much better shape. It is getting better and stronger all the time."

This correspondent used her anger to force changes in her marriage. Sometimes anger is the only weapon that works. However, anger can also be destructive and counterproductive. Humor, assertion, and kindness can be equally useful tools in negotiating new and more satisfying ways of handling change.

Since it is difficult to change old patterns, it is helpful if a woman has some support, either from a therapist or a marriage counselor, or from other women who are trying to make changes. When I was first married at twenty-one, for example, I too did most of the cooking, cleaning, and shopping, even though I had a full-time job. I resented the fact that I worked more than my husband, but I felt guilty about my anger. In 1969, however, after joining a consciousness-raising group, I was relieved to discover that other women shared my resentment.

Within a few months, four of us began to complain to our husbands and petition that they share the household burdens. None of us backed down, and our insistence paid off. Since my husband found that he hated cleaning the toilet as much as I did, his cheerful solution was to hire a cleaning woman. At first, I felt guilty, believing that I should be able to take care of the house myself. This is a common problem among competent women who feel they are neglecting a part of the job their mothers handled alone. However, once I got a little spoiled, my guilt disappeared totally. Having a household helper was terrific, and it made a big difference in our lives. Every woman who works should feel entitled to help.

A husband's willingness to cooperate is a critical factor in redistributing the workload. And for many men that willingness develops slowly. They simply are not used to a life that includes domestic responsibilities. One of my husband's friends once joked, "You can say that women's liberation will benefit men, but I'd like to know how. All I know is that I am changing diapers now, and I never had to deal with shit before. Where are the benefits for me?"

In contrast, Juliet Taylor, the thirty-five-year-old motion picture casting director, who has cast for such movies as Woody Allen's *Manhattan,* has what many would consider a truly equal marriage. She told me, "My husband is like I am. He can't sit and watch someone else do the work. We are pretty role free. My husband always helped his mother and never learned that a father sat smoking a pipe while the wife worked. Really being equal is both of you noticing what has to be done at the same time."

Juliet says she can't imagine living with a man who

expected her to serve him his food or wash his socks. "I see that as childish. A man like that just wouldn't excite me."

Juliet does the cooking and assumes the bulk of child care. Her husband does the organizing and cleaning, takes care of the car, waters the plants, feeds the birds, and is the major troubleshooter with the superintendent. They also have a nanny who helps take care of their son, and lives in two nights a week.

"I've been around couples who fight over whose turn it is to do the dishes," Juliet says. "However, my husband and I are such overachievers, we both offer to do everything. We fight over who is *allowed* to do the dishes."

The Good Marriage

What can we learn from women like Juliet Taylor and other over-thirty wives who have found deep satisfaction in their marriages? As a group, these women seem to share some of the same characteristics.

• They don't dwell on broken expectations or the loss of the romantic ideal of marriage they had envisioned. Instead, they accept the reality and work from there. They are willing to talk things out, express their dissatisfactions, and negotiate a better partnership.

• They know what they want in terms of marriage and career, and they've set up priorities. They recognize that they can't "have it all," and they're willing to make the necessary trade-offs and compromises. They've learned to invest their energies specifically in the direction in which they want to move.

• They have a strong sense of self. They understand the importance of developing and maintaining their own interests, having friends of their own, spending time without their husbands.

• They are willing to give a great deal of time and

care to their relationship, setting aside time to spend alone with their husbands, rekindling their romance in as many ways as possible.

• If they do have problems, they aren't afraid to talk them out or seek qualified help.

A marriage, like any good friendship, does not have to remain stagnant. It should grow, develop, and change as the partners change. As our generation of women come into our own, we can use our strength and newfound confidence to create marriages based on joyous sharing and intimate communication.

One of the saddest sights I've witnessed in restaurants is the long-married couple who have absolutely nothing to say to each other. They sit across the table with glazed eyes, looking totally bored. This does not have to be the role model for our generation's marriages, however. As we experience individual rebirths—returning to school, embarking on new careers, developing assertiveness, we can actively press for rebirths in our marriages.

A necessary step toward marital renewal is setting aside pleasurable time to spend together. The pressure to achieve in the workplace has put new pressures on women, and family life has suffered. Over and over, women complained that they did not spend enough time with their husbands. Without that time it is not possible for a couple to cement their bond and become best friends, which is the essence of a good marriage.

> *A husband is a close friend who really cares. If you have a good relationship, you communicate with each other. I know what offends him, and I don't hurt his feelings.*
>
> *He encourages me in my piano, drawing and*

*painting, and I go sailing with him because he
adores sailing.*

A thirty-six-year-old research
assistant

A thirty-two-year-old woman wrote in to say that she
and her husband had allowed their work to dominate their
lives for several years. They were so busy working and attending night school that they had no time for each other,
and their relationship suffered. Now they are spending more
quality time together and "finding out what we like to do
together."

They have been going to Quaker meetings and discovering "how close we are spiritually." They also have fun
visiting country inns. "We traded in the station wagon my
husband's mother bought for us and bought a Toyota,
which has become a metaphor for both our personalities."
They are also trying to build friendships with a circle of
couples they both enjoy. "Who knows what discoveries we'll
make in the next few years," she says.

Eleanor Smeal, the president of the National Organization for Women, the world's oldest and largest feminist organization, has a superb marriage. She spent her twenties
raising her two children, but when she was thirty, she
slipped a disc in her back and was bedridden. Her husband,
who is her best friend, brought her books from the library.
She began learning about the suffrage movement in the
United States and became interested in women's rights.
When she recovered, she joined NOW and went on to become its first homemaker president.

"My husband," she says, "is as much involved in caring
about social change as I am. I wouldn't have joined NOW if
he didn't join too. We're not the kind of people who like

nightclubs or Caribbean vacations. We don't like to sit. We like politics, work, and children."

The Smeals' marriage works so beautifully because she and her husband share deep mutual interests.

Developing this kind of interest is a proven way to revitalize a stale marriage. "My husband and I began to ask ourselves why we were married," said one woman, who was a career counselor married to an architect. "He had his world and I had mine." Their answer was to take up photography together. Today, two years later, their photographs are displayed all over their home. "We both learned how creative we were," she said. "The experience enhanced both of our identities. We were able to take pride in each other's accomplishments. We couldn't wait to go out and shoot our pictures, develop them, frame them. We became like two kids. It was the best thing we ever did."

Building friendship in a marriage involves encouraging each other's growth. Otherwise, marriage is simply a piece of paper—a meaningless contract. Without pleasure, both parties feel cheated and angry. A successful marriage is a win-win marriage in which the needs of both parties are met.

3

And Baby Makes Three: Motherhood after Thirty

Several years ago newspaper columnist Ann Landers asked her readers whether they would still have children if they had a chance to turn back the clock and do it all over again. Incredibly, 70 percent said that they would *not*. This surprising statistic illustrates, rather graphically, just how much our views on motherhood have changed in the last fifteen years. Although bearing children remains an awesome and joyous event in a woman's life, today it is only one of several choices she can make. The women's movement, the birth control pill, and the easing of traditional values ushered in by the sixties have combined to prove that anatomy is no longer destiny.

But what about the over-thirty woman? For the majority, this freedom of choice came too late. We grew up believing that childbearing and motherhood would be our ultimate fulfillment. We begged our parents for lifelike baby dolls and pretended they were real. We couldn't wait to have children of our own. How then do we explain the results of Ann Landers's informal survey or the many responses I received from unhappy mothers? The answer, in part, relates back to unrealistic expectations. A large percentage of the women I heard from simply didn't expect to find motherhood so difficult, so frustrating, such hard work.

I had children because I wanted them. I didn't think about all the responsibilities. Now I realize how great a challenge and sacrifice having children is for a woman.

A thirty-two-year-old mother

Our mothers lied to us. It makes me furious that they didn't tell us the truth. They should have given us some warning.

A forty-year-old mother of three

My kid hit me like a time bomb. I quit my job, lost all my friends, and grew isolated and miserable. The kid didn't sleep for the first two years. I regained my sanity at thirty, when he was two and a half. Many women regain their sanity when their children are that age.

I like being a mother now, now that I sleep occasionally and don't have to sit in the park all day. As long as he doesn't get sick too often.

My husband and I have decided that one child is almost too much, so I've had a tubal ligation. We might have been happier as a childless couple. Still, having a child is the most complete life experience you can have.

A thirty-three-year-old painter
who had a son at twenty-eight

The majority of mothers in this study had their children when they were in their early twenties, adhering to societal norms and the patterns of their mothers' lives. However, many reported that motherhood did not turn out to be the fulfilling experience they had been promised. To the contrary, many said that motherhood had turned them into "automatons" and "nonpersons"; that they had suffered from depression during the child-rearing years.

> *I've been married fourteen years. I spent the 1960s having babies and feeling depressed. I felt trapped from the time I had my first child at twenty-five. I watched myself become an automaton. I gained fifty pounds I still haven't been able to lose.*
>
> *At thirty-six, I went back to work as the children became older. Finally, I realized motherhood didn't have to be so bad.*

A mother from Massachusetts

> *I had no idea marriage and family would be so much work. I just thought I'd marry and live happily ever after. I had three children, and turned into an angry, dependent housewife.*

A thirty-five-year-old mother

Like marriage, motherhood can be a profound disappointment. A woman gives and gives, pouring all of her energy into this little being whom she herself created. The joy of that giving is supposed to sustain her, nourish her, and for some women, that's exactly what happens. Yet, for others, the constant giving is emotionally depleting and physically exhausting. And because their dreams have not materialized, they become angry and resentful. Some take that anger out on their children; others repress it, feeling guilty for their "selfish" desire to escape, guilty for the ugly, sometimes murderous, feelings they have, which they can confide to no one.

Part of the reason so many over-thirty women suffer from motherhood depression is that many had their children too early, before they had the chance to find out what they wanted and develop an identity of their own. The majority expected to find their identities through motherhood, just as many expected to find their identities through their husbands. However, it is impossible for a dependent, insecure woman to handle motherhood with ease and assurance. She expects to derive a sense of competence from motherhood when she should, in the best of all worlds, have had that feeling of competence *before* she has her children.

New studies indicate that the older mother is often a better mother. Dr. William Granzig, the author, with Ellen Peck, of *The Parent Test: How to Measure and Develop Your Talent for Parenthood*, says, "People twenty-five and above appear to face parenting more *realistically* [author's italics] than those who had children at a younger age.

"On the other hand, women having their first child past thirty-five report a very large percentage of satisfaction. What they lack in stamina, they make up in patience. In contrast, those who had children at an early age expressed far more resentment about the things they had to give up."

The woman who has a strong sense of her own identity, who has proven to herself her competence to cope, is ready to take on the challenge of parenthood. She knows who she is and she likes herself.

A thirty-one-year-old mother told me, "I was afraid to have a daughter when I was younger, because I thought I would make her unhappy, the way I was as a child. But as I started to feel good about myself once I passed thirty, I thought it would be okay to have a daughter, and okay if she turned out to be exactly like me."

It is too late for many women of our generation to postpone motherhood. They cannot send their children back; they cannot repair the past. However, I would hope that our generation of women would be more realistic and honest with their daughters than our mothers were with us.

Although the median age for childbearing is still twenty-two, deferred childbirth is gaining statistically. According to the Natality Statistics branch of the National Center for Health Statistics, the rate of first births to women ages thirty to thirty-four was 7.3 per thousand women in 1970. Yet by the end of the decade, there was a 5 percent increase.

Late motherhood is less of a medical risk today. "At the age of thirty-six, the risk of mongolism is one in two hundred and fifty," says Janet Price, the author of *You're Not Too Old to Have a Baby.* "It's one in twelve hundred during the twenties. The highest risk is one in forty after the age of forty-five.

"Once a woman gets past thirty-seven, medical experts recommend an amniocentesis test. This can determine birth defects, such as mongolism, and can also be used to determine the sex of the child, when it is done after the thirteenth week of pregnancy. Amniocentesis is what makes it possible to be so optimistic about saying, 'If you want to wait until you are in your thirties, it's okay.' "

Women who have children later in life often find that the joys of motherhood far outweigh the negative aspects. However, this new view brings little comfort to those who suffered and are still suffering from depression and motherhood stress. We must ask what pressures create such stress? What conflicts do over-thirty women experience? Why are some happy while others are not?

Sacrificial Motherhood

An essential part of our "good girl" upbringing was the belief that motherhood entailed self-sacrifice. A good mother always put her child first. A "good girl" mother was not selfish or ambitious for herself, only for her husband and children. She subordinated her own interests and needs in order to make others happy.

This view of motherhood has victimized many women who feel guilty for asserting their own needs, for feeling angry about the sacrifices they are called upon to make. Such feelings, we were taught, mean that we are not good, loving women.

Men, on the other hand, have not been raised with the same psychology of self-sacrifice. Men perform at work, but they certainly do not believe that they will necessarily find fulfillment through their work. If they do, that's a bonus. Men work for money and status. They feel entitled to expect benefits from their work—specific, concrete benefits. They have fought for the right to limit their working hours, to have sick days and vacation days. They have the right to complain about their bosses, their subordinates, without feeling guilty about their anger and discontent. But when women take on the twenty-four-hour-a-day job of motherhood, what benefits can they expect? Many, like Dotty in the following story, can't even get time off.

Born Again at Thirty-one

Dotty came to be a "born-again" Christian out of deep personal need. At thirty, she had three children and was "very pregnant" with her fourth. "I loved those children and wanted every single one of them," she says, but she was overwhelmed by their incessant demands. "I saw myself being very unable to meet their needs."

The "worst time" was five o'clock in the afternoon when she was at the stove, and there were all these little kids screaming for attention. "It was confusion! It was crazy all the time!"

She confessed that she often became impatient and wanted to get away and be by herself. "There was a lot of anger in me."

Her anger created great guilt and torment. "I was struck by my lack of love, and I was disappointed I couldn't overcome it." She had an ideal picture of the kind of mother and wife she *ought* to be, and she was in despair because she couldn't reach that ideal. "What was foremost in my mind was the feeling that I was failing as a wife and mother. I didn't like myself very much. There was something wrong with me as an individual."

The situation reached a climax on a beautiful fall afternoon she will never forget as long as she lives. She was pregnant and due any day. She was sitting on the terrace outside, and her husband came home for lunch. He complained that the children were being noisy, and she went out onto the lawn and wept for forty-five minutes.

"I desperately needed help. I had a fourth child coming and I couldn't be the mother I wanted to be to the other three. And now my husband had to put up with my immaturity and crying."

A woman neighbor came to her rescue after the baby was born by giving her a book to read called *Beyond Ourselves* by Catherine Marshall. Dotty read the book and discovered "the key to a whole new life."

Whether it's religion, needlepoint, or volunteer work, the over-thirty full-time homemaker must give herself time off to develop and pursue her own interests. For Dotty the church was salvation, not simply because it brought her peace of mind but because it was a legitimate way for her to get out of the house and spend some pleasurable hours in the company of other adults. The pursuit of pleasure is a valid and necessary part of life, particularly for the woman who spends most of her time chasing after and caring for young children.

One thirty-two-year-old homemaker told me that when she lived in a garden apartment complex with other mothers, she went through a difficult period. "You could never have a conversation with another woman—it was always, 'Mommy, this, Mommy that.' We could never be people. We were always being someone's custodian, either cleaning up after our kids, or cleaning up after our husbands, or cooking dinner or making love—doing something for somebody else.

"One girl said, 'Let's get together one night and play Mah-Jongg.' We all went, 'Mah-Jongg. Ugh!' None of us knew how to play so we got together and learned. It was fantastic because for the first time we could just be together without being our husbands' wives or our kids' mothers.

"We would get together one night a week and play until four in the morning—we were basket cases the next day. It was great. There were about eight of us, and we'd be falling on the floor and laughing. We needed that. That's when I started to look at myself and realize that I needed to do more than take care of somebody else. I had to take care of me. I didn't think that was a selfish thing. I felt I owed it to myself as a human being, although I couldn't put it in those words then."

The Joys of Motherhood

Women who are physically able to have children take that privilege for granted. Perhaps it is important, therefore, to listen to the voice of a woman who has been yearning to have children and hasn't been able to conceive. "I want to perpetuate our line of women—my mother, my grandmother, my sister, myself. We are all bright, sensitive, loving, alive, vital, strong, and mystical women. I feel the world should have an extension of us. I hope to have a daughter because I believe women are often superior, spiritually and emotionally, to many men."

Pam has undergone two extraordinarily painful operations to become fertile. "When I talk to my friends, they say, 'What are you doing this for?' I ask myself that. Intellectually, it doesn't make any sense. I have a comfortable life and freedom. My husband has two children from a previous marriage and isn't crazy about having more. I have to think that the maternal drive is an animal biological instinct."

I believe that one of the strongest drives behind motherhood is the need to bond with our own mothers. This is something rarely talked about in our culture. In fact, the gap between adult women and their mothers has been widening since the decline of the extended family. The "biological instinct" may be, in part, a need to transcend that gap. Through childbirth a woman can repeat and share her mother's experience.

"A mother only gets her daughter back once she has children," a woman who was unhappy about an adolescent daughter's rebellion once said to me. Mothers quickly recognize the agonies their own parents have suffered, and, as a result, they often feel less angry and more loving and understanding.

> *I didn't realize until now what a wonderful mother my mother was. It's not easy to have a baby and she had two. I wish she were here, and that I could share the baby more with her.*
>
> A new thirty-two-year-old mother

As I talked to many women for this study, I heard the same simple eloquent words, "I love being a mother." Motherhood allows these women to express deep nurturing drives.

The wonderful thing about children is that they are so much fun and bring out the child in us. Kids make us forget our troubles and help us remember how to laugh. "We're playing hiding under mommy's skirts," a friend once giggled into the phone when I called her to chat about US-USSR relations. With her five-year-old daughter, she had escaped into a private imaginary world. I was the one worrying about the impending nuclear holocaust. She wasn't. Instead, she was implanting values and ideas, proof of her belief in the future. In the face of death, she created life.

Motherhood without stress can be one of the most joyous aspects of a woman's life. The privilege of living with children should not be underestimated. A prominent psychiatrist told me that she feels there has been too much emphasis on career fulfillment lately and not enough on the joys of motherhood. She has three sons, and if she were forced to choose between her children and her career, she would choose her children. "The rewards are different and more lasting," she said.

It is certainly true that in the last fifteen years, the role of full-time mother has lost much of its former prestige. Today, women are encouraged, exhorted, and expected to raise children and work outside the home as well.

This new pressure has angered many traditional homemakers. They feel they are misunderstood because they choose to be full-time mothers and wives.

Thirty-four-year-old Leslie, for example, is married to a successful lawyer. She and her husband have two daughters, ages ten and twelve, and own a comfortable home in a suburb outside of Cincinnati.

"Last year," she said, "since my children were older, I thought I would return to work. I bought a few new dresses and began to do some substitute teaching. I hated it. It *wasn't* fulfilling. I found myself thinking, I get such tremendous satisfaction from my own children, so why do I have to look for fulfillment outside, teaching other women's children?" She sighed. "Working was such a rat race. Getting up in the morning, rushing to work, rushing home to cook dinner. I had to ask myself, Leslie, what are you doing this for? You know, I've never been an ambitious person. I've never had any big goals in my life."

If she needed the money, she would have no choice. She would have to teach even if she hated every minute of it. However, her husband earns a good salary and takes pride in the fact that his wife doesn't have to work. And he has ensured her financial independence by putting the house in her name and opening up a savings account for her.

"I'm always busy," Leslie says. "The girls need to be driven to ballet and horseback riding lessons. I have to buy their clothes, take them to the dentist, help them with their homework. There always seems to be something to do. Moreover, as they enter adolescence, they seem to need me more than ever."

How did the degradation of motherhood occur? Who is responsible? Many traditional homemakers blame the women's movement and its emphasis on female independence. Certainly, feminism encouraged many women to reevaluate their lives, to think seriously about developing their talents and involving themselves in the professional world. However, one unforeseeable consequence was that women who did choose to be full-time homemakers were suddenly looked upon as women who had nothing to do.

Somehow everyone suddenly overlooked the fact that the average homemaker spends fifty-seven hours a week working in her home. Leslie, for example, cooks, cleans, irons, and shops. As the wife of an upwardly mobile man, she operates as his assistant, public relations person, and psychiatrist. She entertains his clients. To her children, she is a teacher as well as a full-time nurturer.

Penny, a thirty-four-year-old suburban mother in Harrison, New York, had this to say about her choice. "You know, this is not an easy life. Last week, I hardly got any sleep because my son was sick." She paused. "Just look at me now." She pointed to her blouse, which was dotted with baby spit. "This isn't a glamorous life. It's damn hard work. Don't you think I sometimes say to myself, God, wouldn't it be great to get up in the morning, put on a great dress and makeup, and then go to the office?

"But on the other hand, I *did* work. I did have the experience as a secretary. And working wasn't always so much fun. There are many men who would probably love to stay home with children. I've seen their faces commuting to work, back and forth every day. They look defeated and miserable. Work isn't so fulfilling to them.

"Besides," she continued, becoming more and more passionate, "look at these two children I have." We turn to see Tara, two, and David, five, playing with a Wonder Woman doll. "Who is going to take care of these children? Why should they be brought up by someone else? Children need a tremendous amount of care and understanding and time. Like all human beings, they thrive on love. Love is the answer to the problems of the world. Not careers. Love."

Besides caring for her family, Penny devotes fifteen hours a week to the Catholic Church, counseling unmarried, pregnant teenage girls. She also lectures to adolescents on the dangers of drugs, alcohol, and premarital sex.

"Volunteer work is the backbone of America," she says. "I want to help these girls. Don't tell me that just because

I don't receive a paycheck, what I'm doing is not important."

Penny and Leslie are only two examples of many, many homemakers who do receive fulfillment from the work they do. And this does not mean they will suffer from the empty-nest syndrome in their menopausal years. Once their children leave the nest, they may find new dreams, return to school, or begin to develop a career.

For now the work they are doing is of the highest importance because they are raising the new generation. "Why should I let someone else raise my children?" the mother of a bright three-year-old daughter asked me. "How do I know the woman I hire will love music the way I do and teach my daughter to love music?" Her question makes perfect sense, especially because it is becoming increasingly difficult to find qualified household help. Many working women are forced to hire uneducated women to take care of their children. Will their children be able to compete successfully with Leslie's child, who gets straight A's in school, thanks to the loving guidance of her mother? This is a question many women today might ponder as we come to terms with women's and children's needs in the 1980s.

The Superwoman Mystique

Betty Friedan published *The Feminine Mystique* in 1963 and exploded the myth that American housewives were finding joyous fulfillment in waxing their floors, cleaning their homes, and taking care of their husbands and children. Now, only seventeen years later, we're trapped at the other end of the spectrum, fighting an equally destructive myth— the superwoman mystique. Somehow we lost sight of the middle ground.

The superwoman handles a career, her domestic responsibilities, and child rearing with ease. She's very popular with the media, but she's not as easy to pin down in real life. The women I heard from tell a very different story.

> *I always wanted two children, but having one made me realize I'm not willing to make the career sacrifices a second child would add to those I'm already dealing with. I wish I could reconcile my guilt over wanting to be with my colleagues more than with my child.*
>
> A thirty-one-year-old

> *I think anything is easier than being a working mother—a priest, an astronaut, anything!*
>
> A social worker at the Jewish Family Service Agency in Brooklyn, New York

> *The pressures in my marriage are that I kill myself getting things done, while all my husband does is sleep. Complete responsibility for three children has been known to turn me into a raving lunatic.*
>
> A thirty-four-year-old mother

Hardly anywhere in the media is there acknowledgment of the impossible workload the working mother carries or the despair that she feels. Many women who try to juggle both career and family feel like the woman above who described herself as an occasional "raving lunatic." There are never enough hours in a day, too many demands without any rewards, and no time for a woman to replenish herself. Many women, especially those who receive little help from their husbands, feel as if they are on an endless treadmill. This is especially true for those who have uninteresting jobs as opposed to satisfying careers.

Nowhere is this more true than when we look at the plight of single mothers. Single motherhood, for many, is a lonely, exhausting, and often thankless task, as women report over and over.

> *I struggled with two children, part-time work, and dating, the year I was thirty-one. When I was thirty-two, my daughter started school, the little one was in nursery school, and I could begin my career in earnest. However, the demands of mothering and working were often depressing. I struggled to stay on top of things.*
>
> A thirty-seven-year-old real estate broker in Atlanta, Georgia

> *The most difficult part of being a single mother is that you have no one to share your problems with. Plus, you're always exhausted. I feel disappointed in motherhood. I feel my children do not appreciate me, or realize all I have given up for them.*
>
> A thirty-six-year-old government worker in Meridian, Mississippi, with three teenagers

> *I don't recommend single parenthood. It's very hard. I have no relatives, parents, brothers, sisters, cousins, or steady boyfriend to discuss the problems that come up on a day-to-day basis. My husband lives out of state and remembers the children with a note at Christmas. When I speak of single parenthood, I really mean single.*
>
> A thirty-six-year-old medical technologist

I'm tired and slightly resentful that I do all the work, and every other weekend my husband gets to be the fun parent.

> A thirty-three-year-old divorcée who works full-time, goes to school at night, and cares for a nine-year-old and an eleven-year-old

Single working mothers hardly ever receive recognition: theirs is an isolated, heroic, unsung struggle. Although divorce has brought new freedoms to women, it has also placed on their shoulders heavy burdens that their foremothers did not have to bear.

In the past, women lived in extended families: There was always a mother, sister, or aunt who would help out. There was a network of support. Today, however, many of these traditional supports have disappeared. Women either have to work or want to work, yet many are receiving little help for their efforts, either from their husbands, ex-husbands, or society in general.

Many over-thirty mothers embrace the superwoman mystique as fervently as their mothers embraced the feminine mystique. Because they've won the right to work outside the home, they don't realize that they're still being victimized by unrealistic expectations. Just as our mothers assumed that other women were all paragons of domesticity, these women assume that their peers are juggling their myriad responsibilities with grace and ease. Consequently, most suffer silently, feeling guilty and frustrated about their apparent failure as women. We are indeed our mother's daughters! Total woman or superman, the legacy of female guilt endures.

Dr. Nye (a pseudonym) is a well-known professional

who had her first child in her thirties. Her supposed adeptness at role juggling would make her a natural to grace the pages of a woman's magazine. It was because of her image as superwoman that I chose to interview her. However, superwoman was not feeling well the Monday I visited her. She was exhausted, unkempt, and irritable, even though it was only eleven o'clock in the morning.

"What's the matter?" I asked. "Didn't you sleep?"

"My daughter is only four months old," she said. "I've never been so tired in my life." She paused. "I didn't even have time to wash my hair this weekend. This is my last child. I can't go through this again."

"I'm glad you warned me," I said.

"Oh," she said, completely changing her tune, "believe me, it's all worth it."

This abrupt reversal, the result of conflict and guilt, came as no surprise to me. I had heard it many times before from women who simply had not expected, or were not prepared for, the drastic changes in routine and life-style precipitated by a baby's arrival. Many assume, especially if they have outside help, that their lives will go on much as before. As one new mother told me, "I had my baby and expected to be back in the office three weeks later. But I found, to my astonishment, that I didn't want to go back. I felt jealous of the baby-sitter. I didn't want to leave my baby with her. I experienced strong, possessive, powerful emotions I never expected to feel."

It is vitally important for over-thirty mothers to realize that having a baby will change their lives. Some will discover that they want to be full-time mothers; others may find that role too limiting. In either case, feelings of guilt are psychologically unhealthy and counterproductive. It's time to do away with the model of self-sacrificial motherhood in any form. Whether we aspire to be traditional mothers or superwomen, the element of female sacrifice in both images is an unrealistic yardstick by which to measure ourselves.

Parents as Partners

There are women, of course, who manage to combine motherhood and work with a minimum of stress. These are women who have: (1) the money to afford help; (2) fulfilling careers that build their confidence and self-esteem; and (3) husbands who share totally in the child-rearing process.

Brenda Feigen, for example, is a thirty-six-year-old lawyer. Five years after her marriage to lawyer Marc Fasteau, she had her first daughter at thirty.

"I love being a mother," she said. "Alexis goes to school from nine to three. We have a housekeeper who picks her up from school and is with her until we get home at about six. Marc and I totally share caring for our daughter."

Motherhood, she feels, has brought out her nurturing capabilities. "I never really was nurturing before. I'm definitely a grown-up now. We can never do something like sleep all morning. Not that either Marc or I would! You're always on call, even if you have someone living in."

Her energies, she told me, are now focused on her career and daughter. "My husband and I don't seem to have to protect and preserve our relationship in an active sense. I don't have to spend a lot of psychic energy on it."

Her friendships, however, cannot occupy the space they once did in her life, a common complaint among working mothers. "I find myself going for a month or two without seeing friends. I no longer expect to have dinner with my friend Gloria once a week or run over every time I'm happy or sad. I miss the freedom I had. I would like to have it all. But I know I can't, and I've made my choice."

Close Encounters with a Baby

Lynn Grossman is a thirty-year-old television writer. Her husband, Bob Balaban, is a thirty-two-year-old actor-writer who played in the movie *Close Encounters of the Third Kind.*

Bob and Lynn have been best friends since college. Bob bought her a baseball mitt for her twenty-eighth birthday so they could play ball together in Central Park during the summer. When she was interviewed, they had just had their first baby.

"Having a child is such a fabulous experience," Lynn said. "But I'm tired all the time. It took me two weeks to realize you can have a baby and still wash your hair every other day. The first time Bob and I tried to make love, we fell asleep in each other's arms, we were so exhausted."

Parenthood is a totally shared experience, since neither Bob nor Lynn leave their home to go to an office. "The hardest thing about having a baby is scheduling. We have a Bob and Lynn list in the kitchen. This is what I have to do, this is what he has to do, and this is what we do together.

"It's so wonderful to share everything all the time. I sometimes get lonely when I go shopping by myself. We love to do our marketing together, we love to cook together, we love to take care of the baby together.

"There's something about raising a child. The other day I was going to meet Bob at two-thirty on the corner of Sixth Avenue and Ninth Street. Bob was standing across the street with the baby in front of Balducci's food store. I smiled at him and he smiled at me. It was the happiest moment of my life! That made me happier than when I made my first network sale, which *had* been the happiest moment up until then. I felt a certain warmth from my head to toe. It was a religious experience."

However, women whose husbands totally share in child rearing are still the exception rather than the rule. In our culture men have not been encouraged to be involved fathers. Men of our generation were taught that there was a very clear distinction between man's work and woman's work. Ambitious men, moreover, often feel compelled, in their twenties and thirties, to put long hours into climbing the corporate ladder. They, too, face a conflict over where to put their energies. One thirty-year-old working woman I talked to wanted to have a child, but she expected her husband to share equally in the work. However, he was just finishing a degree in law and knew he would have to put in fifteen-hour days at the law firm he would join if he was to compete successfully. He didn't feel ready to take on the commitment of a child. His wife felt that family life was more important, but he was ambitious. They now face a conflict that they do not know how to resolve.

Many men and women who grew up with uninvolved fathers regret that they never really had the chance to get to know their fathers. Some go so far as to question whether or not they were really loved. "My father never fathered my brother or myself in any way," one thirty-two-year-old reporter said, "except that he provided us with material comforts."

Some American fathers offer only authoritarian guidance in the home. Their children fear them. Several single mothers reported that they were happier without their ex-husbands around because they and the children were more relaxed without the man's demanding presence. "My husband would come home from work and start giving orders," one woman complained. "I felt reborn when we got a divorce and I didn't have to listen to him anymore."

According to the experts, the absentee-father syndrome can do great psychological damage to a child. Dr. Abraham

Maslow writes, "We postulate that juvenile violence, vandalism and cruelty implies a hostile and contemptuous lashing out in understandable retaliation against the weak adults who failed them. We feel this to be directed more towards the father than the mother."

How can we encourage our men to become more involved humanistic parents? Women's magazines could play an important role here in directing child-care advice to both mothers and fathers. Similarly, television could offer nurturing role models for men. We see cops, detectives, and other macho types by the dozens. But how often do we see a portrait of a loving involved father?

While we seek greater support from our men, we must also fight for social innovations to make that support possible. For men to become truly involved fathers, business has to become much more flexible about allowing men to work fewer hours, especially when the children are young and need almost constant care. Paternity leave, quality part-time jobs, play-care centers, and flexible hours are important for both men and women in the 1980s.

Motherhood stress will never be alleviated until women feel entitled to demand new support structures from their society.

In view of some of the problems we've seen, what are women doing to alleviate motherhood stress and make the experience more pleasurable? The following findings emerged:

• Women who report the greatest satisfaction do not allow themselves to feel guilty about asking for help from their husbands, friends, and relatives. They don't delude themselves into believing that they are the only ones capable of caring for their children. They recognize the importance of meeting their own needs as well.

• When they are exhausted, they sit down. They teach

their children to respect their wishes; they don't allow themselves to become slaves to their children. They encourage older children to handle chores on their own; they ignore sloppily made beds and mismatched dishes on the dinner table. They expect their children to honor their requests for uninterrupted private time in which to pursue their own activities.

• They spend at least an hour a day having fun with their children—cuddling in bed, working together on a project, enjoying a walk or a bike ride.

• Most are not authoritarian mothers; rather they are friends with their children—a style that differed radically from the way they were raised. They rarely, if ever, resort to physical punishment. They are loving, they laugh a lot, and they relax with their kids whenever possible.

A divorced mother in Florida wrote, "My daughter and I talk constantly about our feelings. I feel a bond with her I never felt with my own mother. I feel more open, loving, honest, and hopeful because of my daughter. Next to finding my own life, my daughter is the most precious thing in the world to me."

Thirty-seven-year-old Betsy Osha, who works for ABC-TV's "20/20" in Manhattan, says, "I like to hug my children and have those little bodies in bed with me. My kids are so interesting that I wouldn't like anyone who didn't care for them. I'm not a very authoritarian mother. You can't not be around and then go home and boss them. You have to be able to take joy from the relationship."

The mother of a fourteen-year-old said that dealing with her adolescent daughter had become a terrible strain. To ease the tension she signed up for a jazz dance class with her daughter. "I wanted to get out of the mommy role and just be a person with her," she said. "We laughed and had a lot of fun in class. It broke the ice between us."

Finally, most happy mothers reported that they had a

strong support network and close bonds with other people. One woman found a widow to live in with her family when she went back to work. Another found a college student to help the children with their homework. Single mothers who managed well were those who had set up a cooperative relationship with their ex-husbands or worked out joint custody agreements.

This can sometimes be difficult for couples, since children often become one of the main weapons in their battles with each other. As one woman said, "The reason my husband and I divorced is that we couldn't get along during our marriage. How are we supposed to get along now that we are divorced?"

However, as divorce therapist Catherine Napolitane and I said in our book, *Living and Loving After Divorce,* women should remember that it is often in their best interests to establish a cordial relationship with their ex-husbands, at least when it comes to the children, and fight for their rights to have their men share in child-care responsibilities. And such a relationship is certainly in their children's best interests; no child wants to choose between mother and father.

Bonding with other women is equally important. One thirty-two-year-old mother has to travel for her job every other week from September through May. She is able to do this because she shares her apartment with another single mother.

Women must work at making motherhood easier and more fun. Five single mothers, for example, could bond together and share cooking responsibilities. A different woman could host the group each night of the week, allowing the others a night off. This would also be an excellent way for a woman to provide adult company for herself. Once women feel entitled to pleasure in motherhood, they will begin to discover creative solutions for their problems.

CHAPTER
4

The Unmarried Woman and the Singles Crisis

Shortly after my first husband and I separated, I went out to Long Island to spend Easter Sunday with my family. It was the first time in a decade that I was spending this holiday without my husband.

I woke up in my cramped studio apartment alone, got dressed, and caught the train to Long Island. My father met me at the station. I felt like a little girl; without the protection of my husband, I was once again my father's daughter. There was no other man in my life.

It's not easy to be single in our society particularly for the over-thirty woman. She's looked upon as an old maid, a misfit in a coupled-up society, too unattractive or neurotic to "catch a man." These attitudes set the stage for the singles crisis we see among over-thirty women who have never married.

I'm going to commit myself to a mental institution if I don't get married by the time I am thirty-five.

A thirty-one-year-old Manhattan secretary

The thought of being alone eating cat food at age seventy terrifies me.

A thirty-nine-year-old stewardess for Delta Airlines

My mother was married when she was twenty-one. Why can't I find a husband?

A thirty-three-year-old stockbroker

I keep thinking of myself sitting in a bathtub with a broken hip, and there's no man to pull me out.

A thirty-seven-year-old office manager

"Women go through a crisis in their thirties," agrees Nancy Archibald Douglas, who earned a Ph.D. from the U.S. International University with a dissertation on the attitudes of single men and women in their thirties. "They feel they have to be married or they will have failed as women. Men do not experience a similar crisis."

The Old Maid Blues

Togetherness was the American dream for the generation of women who grew up in the 1950s. Barbie had Ken; Lucy had Desi.

We expected marriage. When our daddies sat us on their knees, they didn't say, "Now Mary, when you grow up, you're going to live in a brownstone studio by yourself. There will be no one there to kiss you good morning. And you will spend Saturday evenings watching TV by yourself."

What Daddy said was, "Mary, when you grow up,

you're going to have a whole line of boys who want to marry you because you're so pretty and so sweet."

Of course, we believed daddy and the fairy tales we read. Prince Charming would find us, recognize us, and give us his name. That would be our final—and finest—achievement.

> *My mother told me that when I grew up and met the right man, I would live happily ever after. I think her generation had to hang on to that myth because it was lifesaving for them to do so. I think our generation is suffering because we are finding out the myth isn't true.*
>
> A thirty-eight-year-old hockey fan in Santa Monica, California

> *My mother keeps asking what's wrong with me. She is devastated that I'm not providing her with any grandchildren and passing on the Jewish religion. If I stay home on a Saturday night, it drives her crazy. "Go out," she tells me. "Even if you don't like the boy, go out and be seen!"*
>
> A thirty-two-year-old Jewish teacher

The Picture Has Changed

However, Prince Charming is going to be a lot harder to find in the 1980s. According to William Alonso, director of Harvard's Center for Population Studies, "This generation of women now in their thirties will face a very difficult situation if they want to marry in the next few years. The ratio of available men to women is very small. There are fewer men born, and many of them are married.

"The baby boom started in 1948–49 and peaked in 1959. So those people would now be around thirty. Each successive year during that period, more babies were born. Let's say on the average, women marry men two years their senior. So there are fewer men, since they were born earlier on in the baby boom, than there are women. Once you pair off the marrieds, *the ratio of single women to single men is much larger than the ratio of total women to total men. It's a very unfavorable marriage market.*"

Noreen Goldman, research associate in the Office of Population Research at Princeton University agrees. "Women who are caught just at the upswing of the birthrate are in the most trouble because they end up having to marry men older than they otherwise would have. Of course, there aren't enough to go around. The problem is that marriage patterns are so resistant to change. Women usually marry men two or three years their senior. The women born in 1947 would look to the men born in 1944 or 1945, only to find that there are very few, relative to the women at the forefront of the baby boom."

The result of our complex demographic situation is that *four out of every ten women who are still single at thirty will never marry.* And we can already see the effects of this changing reality in the type of living arrangements we're making today.

• In 1976, 42 percent of all new households in the United States were singles. Only 13.5 percent were couples.

• From 1970 to 1976 the number of individuals living alone increased by 38 percent according to William Alonso.

• A major factor is the rise in the divorce rate during the last decade. Divorce made its largest leap between 1970 and 1976, and a record number of divorces are occurring after fifteen years of marriage. The median age of the average divorcée is thirty-six. Divorce is no longer a rare disease among our generation but an epidemic. As anthropologist-writer Margaret Mead predicted, serial living arrangements are becoming more and more of a reality. Five to ten percent of women thirty years old today will be divorced *twice*.

In short, we are no longer living in the coupled-up world of the 1950s. "Today, there is a greater number of transitions in life states," says Larry Hirschorn of the University of Pennsylvania. "The prototypical family stopped being the majority household type after 1960." Because these changes are so new and so revolutionary, many women have not yet learned how to live alone with ease and comfort.

A friend of mine, for example, almost did not attend a New Year's Eve party thrown by an interesting architect because she did not have a date. Many women still find it embarrassing to arrive at social events without an escort. We feel inadequate because we are alone, assuming that others view us as spinsters and old maids.

"The unmarried man has not been subjected to social ridicule to the same degree as the unmarried woman," says Nancy Archibald Douglas. "If anything, his exploits, whether in the bedroom or on the western frontier, have been glorified in the media.

"It would seem that women, being more sensitive to the expectations of society that they marry young, have gone through a crisis period in their lives when they had to resolve the issue for themselves. The men, not being under the same pressure, do not give the impression that they have been through a crisis which forced them to come to terms with their singleness."

The historic disparagement of single women is a direct result of centuries of social, economic, and sexual powerlessness. Before the Industrial Revolution an unmarried woman was a burden to her family—a useless creature who couldn't work or fulfill her primary function of bearing children, preferably male, to bolster the family fortunes. Some of these women escaped their fate by going into domestic service as maids or governesses. The term *old maid* dates back to this era—a time when few people lived past the age of thirty-five.

The age of industrialization opened up some new opportunities for single women. Factories needed workers, and young women without prospects of marriage grabbed at the chance to support themselves, working sixteen hours a day, six days a week to earn two or three dollars. The term *spinster* came into our language in the early 1800s to describe these women who worked at spinning wheels in the cotton mills.

The single man, on the other hand, faced none of these limitations. Because he had economic freedom, he also had social and sexual freedom. He could appear in public alone without fear of ridicule. He could dine alone and attend social functions without an escort; the unchaperoned woman could not.

These attitudes, unfortunately, still carry a great deal of weight today. Many of the single women in this study reported that they received very different treatment when they dined alone in restaurants. They are often seated near the kitchen or the bathroom, subjected to unpleasant odors and the noise of clanging dishes. Other women reported that they still felt very uncomfortable entering a bar alone. Men tend to assume they're on the prowl, perhaps even prostitutes. Nobody ever assumes that the poor working girl might want to nurse a solitary drink by herself.

The single man, however, is free to pursue all the pleasures of life. He is a bachelor, not an old maid; a playboy, not a spinster. To date, we have few, if any, images of a life of pleasure for a single woman. Without adequate language or images, we have no role models.

The Singles Crisis

The women who suffer the most are those who have never developed an adequate sense of self. Being alone proves to them that they are unlovable and unattractive. They are as fragile as Limoges teacups, only content when they have a man sharing their bed. They suffer from man-addiction, and when they do not have their masculine "fix," they are miserable. For the woman raised to believe she is incomplete without a partner, crossing over thirty simply exacerbates her terror.

I have a friend who, at thirty-eight, has won a reputation as an outstanding painter. She rents a lovely two-bedroom apartment on a fashionable city block. When she divorced at thirty-three, she was certain she would find Mr. Right.

"My first marriage was made when I didn't know my real needs or capacities," she told me. "I believed that I was in a much better position to find the man of my dreams because I had more confidence. I thought men would be banging down my door."

The reality, however, was that she had over fifteen relationships with various men over the next five years, none of which ended in marriage.

"I'm thirty-eight now," she added. "Aging has depressed me. More and more I am coming to face the idea that I may not get what I want. This is what wakes me up in terror at five o'clock in the morning—my basic state as a woman alone, without love, children, or connection. I have a void I can't fill."

My friend has spent a tremendous amount of energy trying to fill that void in her life. She made a conscious, assertive effort to widen her social circle. She continued to pile one brick upon another in her career pyramid. She bought new clothes, paying special attention to the kind of image she wanted to create. "I'm looking more glamorous" she would say with confidence. Yet there were other days when she would stare at the mirror in despair, cursing the bags under her eyes. Aging as a woman alone had brought on a crisis of magnitude, one that sent her fleeing to bed with nausea, inertia, and depression.

She was, my friend, another singer of the old maid blues.

The Biological Deadline

Part of the pressure on the over-thirty single woman is that she's fast approaching the end of her childbearing years. This deadline creates enormous stress for the many unmarried women who yearn for children.

> *I was sure I would have gotten my life in order by now, so that I could have a child, the little girl I'd always dreamed of having. Every day I'm conscious that I don't have the one thing I've always wanted. I'm desperate enough to have a child without being married, except that I lack financial security. The fact that I don't have a child is the biggest failure of my life!*
>
> A thirty-five-year-old woman
> at an Eastern Women's Center
> Workshop

> *I always assumed I'd be married by the time I was thirty. My mother was married at twenty and had six children by the time she was thirty-two. Although I feel stronger to be thirty and finished with the drifting of my twenties, it's beginning to dawn*

on me that I may not get what I want. Now, a family is my top priority. I will be devastated if I am single too much longer and can't have a baby.

A thirty-year-old woman in Chicago just finishing a degree in social work

In the 1950s I dreamed of a period of adventure, then marriage and a family. Now I'm one of the few women I know who has never married. I didn't notice everyone around me getting married while I played. One day I woke up a freak.

The last four years of my life have been like a roller coaster. At thirty-one I left my job after meeting the man I love and want to spend my life with. For three years he has refused to make a commitment to me. I returned to school to fill time, but at thirty-three I fell apart, recovered, and fell apart again.

I'm a basket case. I feel that if I don't have a baby now, I never will. I make brave plans for a life alone, and then I go in a corner and cry. I hate being single and want to have a family while there's still time. It's dawning on me that my lover and I will eventually split up, and I can't transcend my horror at being alone.

A thirty-four-year-old Santa Monica resident

The over-thirty single woman becomes tired of watering her plants and talking to her cat. She wants to feast her eyes on the loving smile on a little face. She wants to bask in the reflected glory of a child. It is one thing to walk down Fifth Avenue as a single woman on a Sunday afternoon, quite another to push a stroller in front of you as you are walking. Oh, to be able to push that stroller! To be able to walk into Lord & Taylor and buy a little blue or pink or yellow blanket for some adorable creature who will hug you to death and hang on to your every word.

The woman who yearns for children hears the cry "Mommy, mommy" in her sleep. Surely, the single woman thinks, as she stares longingly at the green grass beyond her married neighbor's fence, there is nothing more wonderful, fantastic, exalting, and fulfilling as a baby. Surely nothing is more beautiful or sweet.

Parental Pressure

The over-thirty single woman finds little support for her life-style—particularly from her parents. Even if she's chosen to remain single, she often feels tremendous guilt because she's let her parents down. Her mother will never have the chance to plan that long-dreamed-of wedding or gaze lovingly at her grandchildren.

I met Jean, a thirty-three-year-old native-born Californian, while we were both living in the Arabian Gulf. Jean has tawny-colored hair, a wide smile, and an immediately warm manner. She spent her twenties drifting, traveling, studying. When I met her, she was working as a secretary to earn money for a summer vacation in Greece.

When we talked, she showed me a letter she had just received from her mother:

> *Dear Jean,*
> *I'm so glad, darling, that you're going to spend the summer in Greece. But, Jeanie, don't you think you should come home soon and settle down? You know, the years go by so fast. I think the most terrible thing for any woman is to end up alone in her*

old age, without any security or children. Think
about this, Jean. We're all not getting any younger.

"Maybe my mother is right," Jean said. "Maybe I'll regret not settling down when I'm older. But I just can't see it right now. A group of close friends made a pact last year—that none of us would marry. But there's always the fear that somebody will marry, then another friend will marry, and that you'll be left all alone."

She stared down at her mother's letter, lost in thought. . . .

A Different Generation

Like so many of us, Jean feels tremendous conflict about the choices she's making. She loves the freedom and adventure of her life, but she is, after all, her mother's daughter. Will she, she wonders, regret not settling for safety and security? Will she end up miserable and wretched, living out a lonely old age? These are the questions she and millions of other over-thirty women are grappling with as they attempt to resolve their singles crisis.

Resolving the Crisis

Because we are pioneering a new life-style, our journey is particularly painful and confusing.

In the early stages of this study I was discouraged by the data I was seeing. Were there any heterosexual single women over thirty who were happy, I wondered.

However, as more questionnaires poured in, the picture began to change. Women were reporting that they *had* successfully resolved their singles crisis. They were telling me there is such a creature as an independent woman who considers herself whole and complete without a man in her life.

These findings were verified by other professionals.

"Women have a crisis in their thirties because they're not married," states psychotherapist Charlotte Behre, who practices in New Orleans, Louisiana. "However, after a transition period, they relax. Being single is not a problem anymore. Many women don't want to marry ever. Others find they just might marry later."

"From many of my women's comments," agrees Nancy Archibald Douglas, "I felt that they often weathered this crisis in their thirties. They decided they *could* live the rest of their lives unmarried, if need be, without feeling that they were failures or that their lives were wasted."

Listen to the voices of the women in this report.

In my twenties I thought I would marry, but I like my lack of obligation to others too much. I like feeling responsible for myself. I love my freedom. Younger sisters find this hard to understand, which is frustrating. I'm conscious of a need to provide for my old age.

> A thirty-year-old teacher in the Midwest

I feel differently about being single in my thirties than I did in my twenties. Whereas in my twenties being alone still had the stigma of not being chosen, I now accept being single as my choice. I no longer have to go out with men with interesting careers because I have one of my own.

> A thirty-three-year-old interior decorator

In my twenties I thought that if I didn't get married by the time I turned thirty, I'd kill myself. Now I

*feel I can have a very nice life without a husband.
I no longer have to go out on a date just for the sake
of having a date. If I marry, that will be a bonus.*

> A thirty-seven-year-old dress-
> maker and graduate student in
> psychology

The comments of these single women echoed those of
women who had been married once and swore they would
never marry again. About half of the divorced women I
heard from said they did not plan to remarry.

*During my marriage I was continually coping with
my ex-husband's emotional problems and overwhelming demands. Now I'm going into my third
year of single life. It's one battle after another, and
at first I was terrified and panicked. I wanted to find
a man immediately.*

*However, I like the woman I've become and
don't want to go back now. Now that I'm single I am
able to meet more people and make more friends.
I have much more time to do what I want to do. I
don't continually have to compromise or meet someone else's schedule. I will never marry again.*

> A thirty-seven-year-old divorcée

Women change so much in their thirties that they are
often able to contemplate life-style choices that were incom-
prehensible to them only a few years before. These are
women who have managed to achieve profound psychological growth.

*I have spent so much energy developing friendships,
and I have friends in four different social circles. I*

*do different things with each group. I can't imagine
a man coming into my life and just fitting in. The
man would have to be pretty exceptional for me to
make room for him.*

A thirty-eight-year-old reporter
for a Southern newspaper

*My own feelings about my singlehood changed
dramatically as I became older. When I was thirty,
I was as desperate as any newly divorced woman
prowling in a singles bar for instant companionship.
My biggest concerns were How could I meet men?
Was I still attractive? When was I going to remarry?*

*However, the more I developed, the less im-
perative marriage became. I absolutely adored all
the wonderful small freedoms of single living. I
loved not having to answer to anyone. I loved going
where I pleased, when I pleased, with whom I
pleased. I found that as my life grew richer, I had
such a busy social calendar it was hard to find time
alone. Yet how marvelous, on the other hand, to be
able to lie in bed all day with a good book and
having no one looking over your shoulder, making
demands, imposing needs. Ah, blissful solitude.*

A thirty-five-year-old divorced
writer

Furthermore, they share one important characteristic:
They are no longer waiting for Prince Charming to come
and rescue them. Instead, they've accepted responsibility for
their own lives and channeled their energies in positive
ways: They are pursuing careers, developing new interests,
building close and enduring friendships.

The single life-style, moreover, is often preferable for women who are ambitious and have demanding careers. In the fields of medicine and psychiatry, for example, some of the most important contributors have been women who did not marry, such as Hilda Brunch, Anna Freud, Janet Mac-Kenzie Rioch, and Clara Thompson.

And this study shows that, for the most part, the high-achieving women of our generation are single. They have managed to overcome tremendous career obstacles only by fierce devotion to, and concentration on, their goals. According to Dr. Matti Gerschenfeld, "Women get hooked into earning their own money and being independent. They don't have time for traditional family life. This is especially true for those who have high achievement levels, who work long hours, and do a lot of traveling."

"One of the best ways women break out of self-defeating patterns is when their husbands leave them," says Dr. Harold Greenwald, author of *Direct Decision Therapy*. "Usually they have settled for lives of quiet desperation. After a divorce, they discover that there's a whole world out there. I used to feel sorry for women whose husbands left them. Now I find that many women use the opportunity of divorce to start all over again."

The Divorce Experience: From Bryn Mawr, with Love

I heard from one woman who had been a suburban mother in her twenties. She did volunteer work for the Boy Scouts, the church, and her alma mater, Bryn Mawr. When she was thirty-two, her husband's job moved them out West. This was a big upheaval and the turning point in her marriage.

Her husband developed a drinking problem. For a time she coped with her loneliness by becoming confirmed in her church, joining a writer's workshop, and playing tennis.

But those choices didn't work, so she decided to leave her husband. She moved herself and her three children from their luxurious home into a little log cabin. Like most full-time homemakers who divorce, she had little money. Right after her move, she had to have a hysterectomy.

After the worst of her transition, however, she returned to school to become a certified nurse's aide. Today, she works part-time and hopes to have a full-time supervisory job.

This is the way she feels about her divorce. "Having always been afraid of divorce, I've discovered it can be a singularly positive move. I appreciate having so much space to myself, and I find that I allow more to others. I have come to see myself as a more adequate woman sexually and emotionally. I have more male friends and wonderful new friendships with young women. I'm excited about moving forward in the human services field and intend to get a master's degree in public health."

A woman I'll call Claire wrote her story on long yellow sheets of paper, attached to the eight-page questionnaire. When she was thirty, she was living in North Hollywood, California, with her husband and a new baby. She had just learned to drive and felt happy. "I expected to be married forever," she said.

When he was thirty-three, her husband asked for a trial separation because he wanted a period of freedom. She was sure he would miss her and return. She tried to be understanding and had sexual relations with him at his apartment several times a week.

Then she discovered that he had another woman, who happened to be her best friend. She felt cruelly betrayed and contemplated suicide. However, she had a child to care for, so she tried to develop her inner resources. She joined the Science of the Mind Church, submerged herself in metaphysics, and began to meditate.

She sold her house and all its belongings and moved to a small apartment with her young son. She took a job as an office temporary, typing mailing lists into computers. She says she was terribly anxious and uncertain whether she could ever be financially solvent.

Luckily, she was transferred to the public relations department, where she spotted a career field with a future.

At first she was "frightened" to be living on her own. After a year and a half, however, she found she loved the total freedom of it. She does not know whether she wants to marry again.

"I like myself a lot more after my divorce," she wrote. "I had developed a tremendous inferiority complex in my twenties. Now I think I'm someone worth talking to."

The results of this study bolster what Catherine Napolitane found when she began working with divorced women and formed her organization, Nexus. That is, the divorce experience is made up of several distinct stages. The first two or three years after a separation or divorce are, for the most part, quite traumatic, especially if a woman has been married for a long time. During this initial stage many women—and men—suffer from anxiety and depression, even to the extent of developing psychosomatic illness. They experience fear and panic as they pull up old roots. During the first few months after a divorce or separation, even the most trivial decisions seem monumental and terrifying. But as women begin to take control of their lives, deciding how to live, where to live, how to support themselves, feelings of competence emerge. And more often than not, a year or two after divorce most women experience a sense of heady exhilaration, realizing, often for the first time in their lives, that they can make it on their own.

Again and again, I heard from women who reported making enormous growth transitions following their divorces. They worked through their depressions, made new choices, and adapted to their new life-styles. All this takes time and patience.

My husband and I had a temporary separation when I was thirty-four. I was confused, frustrated, angry, self-pitying, and afraid of the future. I ran away from the facts. Suddenly I realized it was time to take care of myself and make the most of my life. I wanted to be happy.

At thirty-six we divorced. I lost fifteen pounds, ran through every conceivable emotion, and looked sickly. Thirty-seven was a year of discovery. I was single again and learning how to cope. I found I did better than expected.

This year I returned to work and hope to be a social worker. I'm independent and eager to try almost anything. I feel peaceful and like being accountable only to myself.

> A thirty-eight-year-old office administrator for a private clinic in the south

I was a typical dependent housewife, and when my husband left me, I thought about killing myself.

After my divorce I was working in the garment district, selling, but I couldn't stand it anymore. I had always wanted to be a teacher, but I never received the education I needed. The older I became the more I realized how desperately I wanted to work with children.

With the support of a woman friend I quit my

*job and went to school full-time. The next year I
found a job as a paraprofessional in the children's
public school and continued my schooling at night.*

*Since I've turned thirty, I feel capable of mak-
ing my way in the world. I know I can be self-sup-
porting. A man is not necessary to my survival in
any way. He just complements it. My God, I can't
believe I can say that. Did I really just say that?*

A divorcée with two children

Women who are undergoing a divorce transition must
expect that it will take them between two to five years to
get themselves back on their feet. They have to learn to
overcome bitterness and anger, to conquer loneliness, and
to adapt to a whole new way of thinking and being.

Yet the point is that women do cope with their anxieties and they do change. While the transition period is
rough, there *are* happy endings.

Blocks in the Transition

What are the major impediments to successful resolu-
tion of the singles crisis? Two doctors who have worked
with single people, Marie Edwards and Eleanor Hoover,
report that many single women have incorporated society's
negative stereotypes. "Like any group that has been constantly ignored or downgraded, singles come to believe what
others say about them. And even though they may not acknowledge it, consciously they behave as if they believe it by
limiting the scope of their existence, by not taking chances
in their personal and work lives, by not really choosing
when they have the opportunity, and by seeing themselves
as only temporary people, not rooted in the present."

Myths about the single life, say Edwards and Hoover,
include:

- All single women want to get married.
- It is easier for men to meet women than for women to meet men.
- All unmarrieds are lonely.
- Single life is hazardous because there will be no one to help you if you are hurt or sick.

"As with all myths," the doctors state, "there is an element of truth concealed in them somewhere, but they do a great deal of harm when all singles are assumed to fit these stereotypes, and *when singles themselves shape their own self-images from them.*"

Unfortunately, many women in our society *have* shaped their self-images from these damaging stereotypes. Consequently, they suffer from man-addiction, and when they don't have a man in their lives, they feel empty and miserable.

Germaine's case is a classic example. She has been depressed on and off for years, but her depression has become more acute since she turned thirty. A struggling free-lance artist, she said she is "happy" only when she is involved in a love relationship. She has had only two short-lived relationships in her thirties, neither of which led to marriage.

"At thirty-seven," she said, "I feel angry, bitter, and full of rage at myself, as well as at the world, for the kind of life I have lived. I absolutely assumed I'd be married and have children. I feel disappointed, tremendously disappointed, even though I don't know whether motherhood would have worked for me."

The rage she feels toward herself for failing to live up to her own expectations or "shoulds" is powerful and constant. She feels like a failure and hates herself. Only by bottling up her anger can she keep going day after day. But this repressed rage is at the center of her ongoing depression and seriously depletes her energy.

Germaine's man-addiction stems directly from the fact

that she was raised according to the "good girl" rules and taught that the core of femininity was pleasing a man. During a meeting with me she said, "I used to be so eager to please. I was so afraid of displeasing a man I rarely opened my mouth. Once I was with a married man on an outing in the woods. He forgot his condoms and wanted to have intercourse. I was frightened of becoming pregnant, so I hitchhiked the three miles into town to buy them. He didn't want to go because he didn't want anyone to see him and tell his wife.

"Today, I would hope I'd have the confidence to insist the man go. But I wanted to make his life easy. I've seen my mother do that. I've seen her wait hand and foot on a man when she is in love."

Germaine's mother taught her daughter little about independence or true self-respect. She hadn't learned it herself.

Is it any wonder that, raised with so little experience in autonomy, single women often feel incomplete and helpless about ordering their own lives?

However, if a woman is to grow and develop her own identity, she must overcome man-addiction, essentially by putting herself—instead of a man—at the center of her life. The ability to live happily and securely without men is the real meaning of female independence. Our relationships with men must be based on desire rather than need. And that can be accomplished only when we establish economic autonomy.

Successful Transitions

The women in this study who made the most successful single transitions were those who had money in the bank and owned property. Money allows room for choices and a rare and wonderful kind of freedom.

Economic independence is a key ingredient of psychological independence. The woman who can't afford to live in a decent apartment or pay her bills is the woman desperate for a man to enter her life and make life possible. As over-thirty women build up their bank accounts, they find they can achieve an independence they only dreamed about in their twenties.

Janet, for example, lived in two small ugly apartments in her twenties. "I never paid much attention to them," she says. "My plants were straggly, and my bedroom didn't even have any pictures on the walls. However, since I've turned thirty, I had to face myself and say, 'Hey, this is your life. When are you going to start to live?'

"I just moved into a lovely new apartment. I went to Bloomingdale's and bought myself a set of blue-and-white dishes that I love. My mother keeps saying, 'Why buy new? When you get married, you'll just have to buy all over again.' But I don't know if I will get married. It's important for me to stop waiting for Prince Charming to enter my life before I begin to live."

Janet has learned an important lesson of single life: Putting down roots increases feelings of stability. Physical surroundings and environment are very important to our mental and physical well-being. A woman who is trying to make a successful single transition should create an environment that reflects her personality, her identity. A woman may discover that she's fascinated by Japanese art or mad about collecting cupids. Any new interest should be explored and, if possible, reflected in our homes. When we establish a home base that reflects our special interests and tastes, we affirm our identities, our belief in ourselves. And we gift ourselves with a safe, secure haven to retreat to when necessary.

It is equally important for a single woman to create and maintain a social life whether or not there is a man in her life. "I make sure I do one or two worthwhile things every weekend," one thirty-three-year-old single woman said. "I go to a concert or visit a museum. I take one course during the week, too."

Entertaining, too, should be part of the life-style of a sophisticated over-thirty single woman. I know a single woman who gives a dinner party every week. She invites old friends and new people she'd like to know better. "I used to be afraid to entertain," she said. "I was afraid of doing things the wrong way. But I studied all the books and practiced, and now I've become an expert."

As women, we often dwell on our emotional lives, without taking into account how much economic powerlessness plays on our fears and deepest insecurities. But how could anyone expect to feel secure without a home, a means of support, or money in the bank?

The Search for New Solutions

Although most single women live alone, many find the loneliness, the absence of daily adult companionship, unbearable. But without a man to share their life, they feel they have no choice. Not so! I was heartened to discover that many over-thirty singles are taking the initiative and setting up alternative types of living arrangements to best meet their needs.

While visiting Pilar Campi, a well-known Long Island psychic, I met two women in the waiting room. One was a brunette, age thirty-four, whose husband had deserted her and her two children. The other was a divorced blonde of the same age who had only one child. Carol worked as a bookkeeper, Jane as an office manager. They lived on the same suburban block.

"How are you managing living alone as women?" I asked.

"It's the funniest thing," said Jane. "Carol and I have become a couple, even though we don't live together. I used to depend on my husband to do the grocery shopping because I hate to do it. Well, Carol does it for me now. I have learned how to fix a car, and I do that for Carol."

She still seemed surprised at their arrangement. It was not one she would have predicted for her life. She and Carol were not lovers but true and deep friends. Knowing they could depend on and trust each other gave them a sense of family, a family not recognized by the census takers, but a family nonetheless.

Deep friendship among women may be new to us because many of us grew up believing women were natural enemies in the ongoing battle for men. However, the companionship that other women can provide can be the difference between happiness and misery in a single woman's life.

For my friends Mitzi and Shelley, living together was the right answer. At thirty-three, Mitzi was raising her son, Josh, alone. Her best friend, Shelley, had gone to London to set up a retouching business. One evening when Mitzi was feeling lonely and overwhelmed, she called Shelley long distance to cry and complain.

When Shelley suggested that she come to London, Mitzi packed her bags and took off. The two women and Josh lived together in a London flat for two years. Shelley was a second mother to Josh, who was the baby she'd always wanted. Josh had two loving females around, and Mitzi had support and companionship.

In the single life a support system can make all the difference. It's important to know that a friend will be there to take care of you when you are sick and make sure you have a place to go on the holidays.

"Old patterns of intimacy in friendships, love affairs, and marriage have been undone in barely one generation," says Perry London, professor of psychology and psychiatry at the University of Southern California. "New ones are not yet developed enough for the forms of contemporary intimacy to be entirely clear. Sexual values are in transition, housekeeping arrangements are in dispute, hurt feelings remain to be assuaged, new means of coping and new protocols for social behavior are in demand."

The Need to Nurture

Single women who want to have children also need broader social acceptance. One thirty-nine-year-old statistician told me she had been seeing a psychiatrist for eleven years in an effort to overcome chronic depression. As she approached forty, she told him that she desperately wanted to adopt a child. He responded by explaining why that would be a neurotic decision—because she didn't have a husband. How could she possibly raise a child by herself?

Unfortunately, this belief is all too prevalent, even among single women themselves. One woman who wrote to me expressed the feelings of many others when she said, "Although I have thought about having a child on my own, I lack the courage to do it. I would be afraid to hinder the normal development of a child. I believe a child needs the love and attention of two parents."

However, many over-thirty women suffer real feelings of deprivation when they cannot express their need and ability to nurture. Moreover, many single mothers do an excellent job of raising their children on their own, in spite of tremendous obstacles.

Adoption over Thirty

It is difficult to adopt a child as a single mother but not impossible. Most agencies prefer couples, and there are long waiting lists for couples who want Caucasian babies. However, adopting a foreign child is an alternative that many single women might consider. An organization called The Committee for Single Adoptive Parents in Washington, D.C., puts out a comprehensive fact sheet on adopting children from foreign countries.

A thirty-nine-year-old actress who does television commercials in Los Angeles worked through this organization and joyfully reported on the children she had adopted, a two-year-old Bengali girl, half Hindu and half Moslem, and an Indian baby from Bareilly, near the border of Nepal in northern India. She lives with them, a housekeeper, and six animals in a small north Hollywood home.

"There's something about having a baby in the house that's so delicious," she raved. "I couldn't be more passionate about my children if they came from my own body. I just always loved the idea of a large family in which everybody was close and loving."

She admits that her life has changed as a result of her new responsibilities. "My life really isn't my own anymore. I have to consider the children before I do anything. I didn't realize how much I treasured my privacy until I lost it. A year ago, when I was in the shower, the door opened, and there was Emily with four of her girl friends. I'm dripping wet and naked, and she's asking me to take them for ice cream!"

Because she has a housekeeper five days a week, she has a great deal of freedom to pursue her career. Yet she finds more pleasure in spending time with the children. "Before the children," she says, "I was more focused on my career. I would really fret about the work I wasn't getting. Now I seldom get upset. If I lose a job, it's okay, and maybe I'll get one next week. My children and the time I spend with them are more important to me."

Having her children has made her feel less desperate about having a man in her life. "If someone were to move in with me, he might become an authority figure and discipline my children. We don't have that here. They're *my* children and I think *I* should bring them up. They don't have anyone they can go to and con into saying yes when I've said no.

"I'm not looking for a man to take care of me and my children. I do very well. I just can't believe somebody else would come in here and do as good a job."

For single women who aren't comfortable with the idea of adoption or single parenthood, there are other ways to meet the need to nurture. During one period in my life I applied to be a volunteer at the New York Foundling Hospital, which is run by Catholic nuns. I would leave my office on Friday evenings, change into a volunteer's uniform, and spend about four hours there, feeding, diapering, and playing with babies.

I always left the hospital feeling uplifted. I needed to be with children and thoroughly enjoyed them. My volunteer efforts were a way of preventing a depression I might otherwise have experienced.

Single women can also take in foster children or become Girl Scout leaders, Big Sisters, or day-care center volunteers. And if single and married women ever begin to form a network, single women could share child-care burdens with overwhelmed married mothers, providing an outlet for their maternal instincts and giving harried mothers a welcome and necessary break.

Where Do We Go from Here?

We lack positive images of the strong, independent single woman, the female "playboy" who can indulge her appetites without guilt. Yet this woman exists, in my imagination. She has a career, which gives her independence. She has a lovely wardrobe, travels when she can, and entertains at least once a week—when she's not attending concerts, plays, and dance recitals. She collects the works of artists and writers she admires. Friends and lovers want to be around her because of her kindness, generosity, and wit. This is the kind of woman I would have liked as a role model for our generation of women when we were growing up.

Now we have the opportunity to create that image, using our freedom wisely because it is so new and so precious.

Only fifty years ago American women were not allowed to vote or to be on the streets at night without a chaperone. Today, we have unprecedented freedom—freedom women in other parts of the world envy.

"How did you meet your husband?" I once asked a twenty-one-year-old Egyptian woman.

"My aunt brought him to me," she said.

Her family had chosen the man she was to marry at nineteen; he was a doctor ten years older than she.

"Could you have remained single?" I asked her. "Is there a place in your society for the woman who does not choose marriage?"

"A woman *has* to marry," she told me. "If you don't, everyone thinks there is something wrong with you. Some women have their husbands chosen for them when they are three years old. And you can't get an apartment by yourself as a single woman. It just isn't done. They would think you were a prostitute if you did something like that."

In her voice I heard a yearning for freedom. Oh to be able to have a room of her own! Her own time! Her own choices! But her future had been chosen for her. She had no voice in her destiny.

Surely American women owe women in other parts of

the world a vision of freedom. American women have a mission—to convey the positive aspects of freedom to women who have been denied the choice of autonomy, women who live in a world in which privilege and choice are still exclusively reserved for men.

This means that we must end the social stigma that plagues the single woman. We must banish the words *old maid* and *spinster* from our tongues and minds. We must fight for the right to be treated as equals in our society. Like men, we have the right to walk unafraid on the streets at night, without the threat of rape. Like men, we have the right to order a drink at a bar without being sexually harassed, to eat at a restaurant alone and be treated with respect. Like men, we must have good salaries and jobs with futures.

Single women can become a powerful political force, as they fight for their rights. There are 27.8 million single women in this country today. We ought to stop apologizing for our status and start learning to enjoy it.

We still believe that a woman who is not married by thirty-five is an old maid. Yet that timetable was devised when few people lived past forty. Furthermore, marriage will not solve the dilemma of living alone in old age. Statistically, women outlive men, so many married women may well be forced to live out the last fifteen years of their lives alone. Therefore, learning to live alone in our thirties can prepare us for the future.

We must eradicate the traditional image of the "normal" family and realize that the nuclear family is only one style of living among many. The single life-style is relatively new, but it is growing more and more popular. The U.S. Census Bureau reports that a trend may be developing toward "larger proportions of persons remaining single throughout their lives."

Once we become flexible about transitional life states

and develop new forms of intimacy and friendship, we will be able to revel in our freedom. With money in our pockets the old maid blues will be banished forever.

CHAPTER

5

Discovering Our Sexuality

When I first began interviewing women about sex, I arrived at each meeting with a long list of specific questions and an equally long mental list of worries: Would women discuss their sexual problems and feelings honestly? Would they discuss the subject at all? Had the years of repression taken their toll, making it difficult for older women to open up about a subject that had been off limits when they were growing up?

I needn't have worried. All of the women I spoke to and heard from were willing—even eager—to talk about sex. For many it was the first chance they had to reveal the mass of conflicting emotions that troubled and confused them. Often I didn't even have time to ask my own questions: The women were too busy directing questions at me. Again and again I was asked: What kind of behavior is expected of a woman today? Do extramarital affairs save or wreck marriages? Does the theory of open marriage work in reality? Is casual sex the new utopia or a male ripoff? How are men reacting to women's new assertiveness? Were other women experiencing the same changes and feelings they were? Were other women having fantastic, fulfilling sex lives? Multiple orgasms? Affairs?

As the questionnaires poured in, a similar pattern emerged. Although all of the women wrote about their sex lives in great detail, there was a tentative, almost bemused tone evident in many of their comments. It soon became obvious that sex for the over-thirty woman is a highly charged complex issue. If there was one dominant theme that emerged from the study, it is this: The over-thirty woman is a victim of massive sexual culture shock. In little more than a decade all the rules about sex have changed, and she, more than any other group of women, is still reeling from the effect of this profound transition in sexual values.

Our Sexual Heritage

In order to understand the tremendous conflicts our generation of women are facing, it is important to look back at the sexual climate in which we were raised. When we were growing up in the 1950s, sex was a taboo subject, inextricably linked to shame and guilt. We had few, if any, images of the pleasurable aspects of sex; certainly our parents seemed to us asexual beings. Even if they told us that sex was a natural and beautiful part of marriage, we saw little evidence to support that view. Very few of us saw our parents kissing or even joking about making love. Instead, we assimilated a whole array of negative subliminal messages: Don't touch yourself there. Don't run around naked; it's not nice. Don't climb on Daddy's lap anymore. Don't push yourself against mother's breasts anymore. Nice girls don't think about sex.

By the time we were old enough to date, our knowledge of sex was spotty—mostly gleaned from quick looks at forbidden books and whispered conferences with friends—but our role was clear. We were the ones who had to set the limits, to say no to our boyfriends, to fight our own burgeoning desires. How well I remember saying penance in Catholic church because I had "sinned" by allowing a boy I liked to put his hand on my breast as we sat in the local drive-in movie.

One woman I talked to said, "The implicit message I got was that sex was taboo. I never talked to my mother about it—I didn't even know if she had sex with my father after I was born. My father used to say to me over and over, 'No cow gives its milk away for free!' Can you imagine! So of course I was a virgin when I got married—and although sex went along with the territory of marriage I never really gave it much thought."

Marriage was the prize—the reward—for those years of denial. Prince Charming wouldn't respect us if we gave in, so most of us held out—at least until we were safely engaged—dreaming of the magical fulfillment our mothers had promised we'd experience on our wedding night.

But, of course, by the time we married the message to deny and inhibit our sexuality was too firmly ingrained. Once again we were brought up short by unrealistic expectations. That wedding night, even the first few years of marriage, did not bring that promised fulfillment. How could it? Good sex, like anything else, is based on experience, knowledge, and practice. Most of us were completely unaware of our own bodies. How could we tell our husbands what we wanted when we didn't even know ourselves. Masturbation was as forbidden and unthinkable as "going all the way." As one woman wrote, "My father told me my fingers would fall off if I masturbated. Can you believe it! And if I ever stayed in the bathroom too long, he'd look at me real suspiciously, as if I'd been doing something wrong."

It was not surprising, therefore, to discover that many over-thirty women considered their twenties to be a period of sexual dormancy. Moreover, most reported that they suffered in silence, convinced that their sexual frustration was somehow their fault; that they were inadequate. Or they were convinced that only men wanted or enjoyed sex—and women were to provide it for the price of marriage. And where could they turn? The sex manuals we take for granted today were not available in the early 1960s. Those of us who did seek advice for our "problem" or questions learned that it was, indeed, our fault.

In 1968, a few years after my first marriage, I went to a local bookstore to see if I could find some advice about my own apparent inability to enjoy sex. The only book available was a paperback called *The Power of Sexual Surrender*, written by a Dr. Marie Robinson, a Freudian. I paid for it eagerly and went home to discover what was wrong with me and what I could do about it.

Dr. Robinson assured me that I was in crowded company, that at least 40 percent of American women were either totally or partially frigid. And she explained that the responsibility for this problem lay with the woman herself. "While a husband may help a woman face the nature of her problem, he cannot, through mechanical means, get her over it. Neither can any man other than her husband."

To solve the problem, Dr. Robinson wrote, a woman had to overcome any anger and resentment she felt toward her husband, or their relationship and "surrender to her feminine role," which consisted of "household work and keeping the children busy."

Unfortunately, playing house cheerfully did not make me orgasmic, and Dr. Robinson's advice had a devastating effect on me. I felt more inadequate than ever, and as I neared thirty, I became desperate to find out why I wasn't sexually responsive.

The Sexual Revolution

Then, in the late sixties and early seventies, the climate suddenly changed. The previously taboo subject of female sexuality became an acceptable—even favorite—topic for research and discussion. As a result of the work of pioneering sex researchers like Masters and Johnson, Mary Jane Sherfey, and Shere Hite, we learned that it was perfectly normal, even useful, to masturbate. We found out that the clitoris, not the vagina, was the seat of the female orgasm, that all women were capable of climaxing, that a woman's capacity to enjoy sex was equal to, if not greater than, a man's.

Sex manuals crowded bookstore shelves, and the popular magazines wrote explicitly about female sexuality. We were encouraged to experiment with new positions, with oral sex. We were told that sex was a normal, healthy part of life, that our inhibitions had no place in the modern world.

Suddenly, women who did not go "all the way" were considered "uptight" and "neurotic." The advent of the birth control pill had eliminated the worry of unwanted pregnancy so there seemed to be little reason for us to continue to say no. The image of the prim and proper 1950s "lady" was replaced by the sexy "chick" of the 1970s, a woman who gloried in her body and her ability to have multiple orgasms. Sex goddesses, each younger and more beautiful than the next, dominated TV and movie screens. Women were encouraged to have affairs, to visit singles bars, to engage in casual sex.

What effect did this sudden and dramatic shift have on the over-thirty women? For some of us, the effect was liberating. For others, the change came too quickly and too late. But for all of us, uncertainty and confusion seems to be a natural byproduct of this rapid transition.

Sexual Awakening

Sally is a thirty-year-old publicist and the mother of a five-year-old son. She grew up in a middle-class suburban neighborhood. As a youngster, she was a Girl Scout; in high school, the class treasurer. She wasn't a particularly ambitious student, but she always worked hard. "I wanted to please my parents," she said, and she did. She was very close to her mother.

After graduation from college, she became a teacher. She married her high school sweetheart—"in a way he was like the boy next door"—and after four years of teaching, she had her first son.

The year after the baby's birth was the worst of her life. She was living in Cleveland; her mother was in Florida. She was lonely and frightened about the responsibilities of caring for a newborn. She suffered from postpartum depression for almost a year. "I'd cry and I was so tired," she said. "I'd look at the baby and think, what's wrong with me, why aren't I happy?"

Her sex life was disappointing. She enjoyed the warmth and the hugging, but she never experienced the earth moving. She and her husband made love once or twice a week, and he was always the one who initiated it.

Two years after the baby's birth she took a job with a public relations firm. She discovered that she was very good at her work and she loved it. As feelings of competence developed, she began to feel differently about herself. She became interested in clothes, discarding her jeans and oversized sloppy shirts for soft flowing dresses that emphasized her figure. "When I was in my twenties, my husband often asked me why I didn't wear sexier clothes that showed off my body. But back then, I didn't feel like a sexual person. I acknowledged that I was married and having sex, but that was separate from me. I would never wear a clingy dress or even a see-through nightgown. I still thought of myself as a little girl. Wearing a sexy nightgown would have been a dressing-up game, like pretending to be Rita Haworth or Greta Garbo while I really felt like Plain Old Sally underneath. But recently I've begun to feel womanly—sensual— for the first time in my life. I just bought my first sexy black nightgown and a glamorous Diane Von Furstenberg dress, and I don't feel self-conscious wearing it."

Her sex life has improved dramatically, too. "I've become a lot more interested in sex, not just as a way of being close to my husband or pleasing him but because now it pleases me, too. I'm beginning to shed some of my inhibitions. I was always very quiet during sex. Tim once said to me, 'Sally, have you died?' I was totally inhibited about making a sound. Now I'm starting to express myself more, telling Tim what I want or like. I'm even using dirty words on occasion." She smiled happily. "I'd never have believed that sex could be so much fun."

Sally's experience is a typical pattern I discovered among women in their thirties. In the fourth decade of their lives, many women reported that they were experiencing a glorious sexual awakening, what one termed a sexual rebirth.

> *I enjoy sex more today. I'm not ashamed to reveal my body to a new lover; nor am I as concerned about my performance the way I was when I was younger.*

> A thirty-one-year-old divorcée with two children

Sex is more free, giving, and experimental today. A lot of that has to do with my second husband of two years. Acceptance and trust levels are high.

A thirty-five-year-old training officer in a veteran's hospital

I enjoy sex more than I did in my twenties because I like myself more now. I feel more poised, more confident. I'm more experienced too.

A thirty-one-year-old Mexican woman

I was very nervous about sex until I was twenty-eight. Since then I have been fortunate enough to have two beautiful relationships. I enjoy sex immensely.

A thirty-three-year-old woman who has just begun a public relations business

I enjoy sex much more in my thirties. I began having orgasms during intercourse at twenty-nine. I am more sensual and sexual and aware of my body and desires.

A thirty-six-year-old social studies teacher, divorced, with a son of fourteen

What accounts for this dramatic increase in erotic pleasure among women in their thirties? Why are so many women reporting that they like sex more than ever?

Sex and Self-Esteem

The single most important reason for the over-thirty woman's sexual development can be traced to her developing sense of self-esteem. Contrary to the traditional Freudian model, the passive submissive woman is *not* the woman who glories in her sexuality and femininity. The results of this study clearly indicate that the self-effacing "good girl" remains the most alienated from her sexuality, her sexual powerlessness only one aspect of the overall powerlessness she feels in her life.

The passive woman sees herself as a victim, able only to dream and fantasize about passion but completely incapable of acting on those dreams. She is unable to take any responsibility for her own life or her own needs. She doesn't believe she's entitled to sexual pleasure; therefore, she never takes any risks.

In contrast, the more powerful a woman feels, the more she will enjoy sex. And the over-thirty woman, simply by virtue of her age and experience, is more likely to have a firmer sense of identity than she did in her twenties. Job-related feelings of competence can also have a tremendous impact.

Thirty-four-year-old Eileen, for example, suffered from postpartum depression when her children were babies, and consequently her sex life suffered too. She was delighted when she returned to school at thirty-two for a degree in marketing. She thought she might feel out of place in school, but instead she found it the most exciting experience in her life. Her feelings of revitalized self-worth enhanced her marriage.

"This is a good time in my life," she mused. "I want my husband to reap the benefits of my good feelings about myself. The way I look at it, sex is a manifestation of what is happening in your life. If there's something wrong with your marriage, it's going to show up in bed. When a woman reaches her thirties, she starts to mature and become more aware of, and happier with, herself. Coincidentally, sex improves!"

As women develop a healthy ego and a strong sense of self that has nothing to do with their role as wife or mother, they become less interested in pleasing men and more interested in pleasing themselves. "Women in their twenties are concentrating on pleasing men and receiving approval from men," says Dr. Mildred Hope Witkin, associate director of the Human Sexuality Program at New York Hospital. "Women in their thirties are learning for the first time to love and please themselves."

This theme came up repeatedly. A twenty-nine-year-old woman wrote, "When I was younger I had the old rape fantasy. You know, the man wanted me and I would submit. But that's wearing thin now and I'm beginning to *want* sex now, to be into it." And a thirty-five-year-old woman said, "I'm not the service station for men that I was in my twenties. Sex now is *for me*—not for them."

In contrast, the woman who seeks her identity in the arms of a man, or men, is not very likely to find what she's looking for. In fact, what she may find is a great deal more unhappiness and pain than she bargained for.

Loretta, now thirty-two, spent the greater part of her twenties hanging around the fringes of the rock world. During those years she slept with over a hundred men. Casual sex became her badge of rebellion against the Establishment.

When she was thirty-one, she picked up a man at a bar as was her habit and spent the night with him. In the morning she left to change her clothes at her apartment before arriving at her office.

As she was walking home at eight in the morning, she asked herself what in the world she was doing with her life.

What was the point?

She called a friend and got the name of a woman therapist. As she told her therapist about the endless time she spent at bars, the therapist ventured that Loretta might be developing a drinking problem and suggested she consider visiting Alcoholics Anonymous. She went to her first meeting, and that was the beginning of her new life.

For the first time she began to let her defenses down and share her pain and loneliness with others. She began to realize that she had never had any self-esteem and that her seductiveness covered up inner feelings of confusion.

Through the support and love she received from friends in AA, she began to love herself, and she finally came to acknowledge that her sex life had been both disappointing and ego-bruising. "Even though I slept with all those men," she said, "I never enjoyed sex. I wanted to please men and was willing to go to almost any length to do that. I thought that's what sex was all about."

In her twenties Loretta typified the male-identified woman who derives pleasure only by pleasing a man rather than herself. Even though a member of a supposedly hip new generation, Loretta still believed the traditional message women have, up until recently, received.

"This is a reflection of our entire repressive cultural approach to female sexuality," says Sanford Jason, who teaches a course in intimacy at the New School for Social Research. "Women have not been taught that they have any intrinsic sexuality of their own. They were only taught to respond—to say yes or no—to male sexuality."

Although the support she received from her AA friends was invaluable in helping her to pull herself together, Loretta firmly believes that getting older had a lot to do with her newfound willingness to face her problems. The questions she asked herself on that morning walk home from her lover's apartment would not have occurred to her when she was twenty-five or twenty-six. Then she was too busy rebelling against the strict upbringing she had had. Although she knew her parents' way wasn't for her, she wasn't independent enough or strong enough to break from them and deal with her sexuality on her own terms. Instead, fearing separation yet wanting autonomy, she rebelled in the only way she could—by toppling every rule at once.

In fact, a major task of women in their twenties who are struggling to deal with their sexuality is to find a way to meld their own values with their parent's values. When we violate parental standards, we may unconsciously feel that we're betraying our parents. And if we're not ready to separate from them completely, to take full responsibility for our own lives, this can be a difficult and painful process.

Unlike Loretta, most women respond by hanging onto those parental standards throughout their twenties, which, in turn, accounts for the period of sexual dormancy many women talked about. Only when they had turned thirty and made the transition to adulthood did most women feel strong enough to break with their childhood, to question the values and standards with which they'd been raised.

Sanford Jason agrees that maturity is a major factor in a woman's sexual development. "The thirties today," she says, "are the beginning of a freeing-up period for many women. This is the time in which they begin to shed the taboos, myths, shoulds and oughts they have been brought up with. They're moving away from the childhood controls of their parents. They're becoming adults. They're beginning to live their own lives. Consequently, they may become more experimental with sex."

Liberation

The women's movement has also had a profound impact on our changing attitudes about sex. As a result of the pioneering writings of women like Betty Friedan, Gloria Steinem, and others, we have slowly come to realize that our seemingly isolated problems are simply the byproducts of years of indoctrination and conditioning. Feminism gave us a rallying point and a voice through which to express our dissatisfaction with the lives we were leading. By affirming our worth and our strength, the women's movement helped us develop the self-esteem so vital to our sexual growth. And by encouraging us to band together and share our common problems, the movement helped us work toward real and lasting solutions.

In fact, it was only when I joined a women's consciousness-raising group that I was able to deal with my own sexual problems. For the first time in my life I talked honestly with other women about my sexuality. And together we learned that our individual sexual problems—masochism, orgasmic dysfunction, performance anxiety, the harboring of sexual guilt and shame, the inability to ask for what we wanted—were shared by other women in the room. We finally understood that we were not neurotic because we had problems, but that like all women, we were in the midst of a struggle to build sexual self-esteem and new ways of relating to ourselves and to our men.

We had been raised to feel ashamed our bodies. We believed that female genitalia was ugly, dirty, smelly; that menstruation was a curse. How could we ask men to love this secret part of us when we ourselves found it so offensive?

Reversing so many years of conditioning isn't easy, but it can be done. As we began to learn about our bodies, our feelings of shame slowly disappeared. At a NOW conference slide show I studied pictures of the female body—I saw what the cervix looked like, what the clitoris looked like. I even bought a plastic speculum for three dollars so I could examine myself. This kind of knowledge fosters acceptance.

For the first time in my life I liked my body, felt proud of it. And the effect of this newfound pride on my ability to enjoy sex was dramatic.

My own experience was not uncommon. A significant number of women reported that, far from disliking their bodies as they became older, as they had expected, they actually liked their bodies more.

> *In my twenties I was ashamed of my body and its functions. I never wanted to touch my breasts or vagina. Now I love my body and enjoy feeling and touching myself.*

A thirty-one-year-old mother

> *I'm proud of being a woman, have a positive attitude about my periods, like my new gray hairs, and know I'm getting wiser rather than older.*

A thirty-seven-year-old
medical researcher

> *I'm more aware of my body, know what I look like, and how to make myself attractive. I'm not stylish or sophisticated, but I can be pretty sexy.*

A thirty-three-year-old
unmarried artist

The body of the over-thirty woman actually becomes sexier—a little-known fact. Sex researchers report that the vagina is filled with nerve endings or "sexy" tissue, called the venous bed capacity. While the chief erotic structures of the male are external, they are both external (the clitoris) and internal in the female. And the internal erectile tissue—the venous bed—is the seat of female sexual spasms or orgasm. As a woman's venous bed builds up, she becomes more sexually responsive. Indeed, the more a woman has sex, the more sensitive to sexual feelings she can become. With this fact in mind, we can look forward to active and satisfying sex lives through our thirties, forties, fifties, and beyond.

We might ask at this point: Why is sexual growth so important?

There are two major reasons. First, sex is a major way to receive pleasure, simple bodily animal pleasure, and people need pleasure in order to be happy.

Second, getting in touch with our sexuality can be a tool in building overall self-esteem. In other words, the relationship between sex and self-esteem is symbiotic; each feeds off and fosters the other. "A woman's sexual power gives every indication of being the inalienable source of her assertiveness," states Dr. Ann Seiden, a psychiatrist with a practice in Chicago. "The woman who is sexually self-confident is more likely to be an assertive woman in daily life. She is not afraid that her assertiveness will reflect badly on her femininity because she is confident of her womanliness. She can be demanding and aggressive and still know she is very much a female."

A thirty-one-year-old secretary in a talent agency said that she has become a much more confident person as her sexuality has developed. She has two lovers. "It's not that John's a good lover or Harry's a good lover," she says, "but that I'm a good lover. I feel more powerful now and that's directly related to my sexuality."

Divorce as a Sexual Growth Experience

Another key finding that emerged from this study is that experience counts. Overall, divorced and single women expressed more satisfaction with their sex lives than did married women. In fact, divorcées *almost always* reported that they received much more pleasure from sexual activity than they did when they were married. Many had their first orgasms in their thirties as they rediscovered their sexual personalities as single women.

> *I realized I didn't know anything about sex until I slept with a few men other than my husband.*

> A thirty-seven-year-old
> divorced second grade teacher

> *I was a virgin when I married, and I was faithful for fifteen years. I've been to bed with two men in the year and a half I've been single, and I enjoy sex more. I've found out how sensitive, caring, and understanding some men can be.*

> A thirty-eight-year-old mother

"Marriage," says Sanford Jason, "except for the more liberal, less traditional marriages, still tends to confine a woman's sexuality. A single woman is exposed to many different men and different ideas. She tends to be more experimental."

A thirty-two-year-old office manager from Chicago , wrote that the year she turned thirty, she lost one hundred pounds and met a man who had many of the qualities she missed in her husband. They began an affair.

His consideration for her feelings surprised her, since "my husband never treated me that way." After three weeks she climaxed—for the first time in her life. She was stunned to discover that her frigidity had not been her problem alone, as she had believed, but a function of the quality of her relationship with her husband.

Once she discovered passion, she "couldn't waste any

more time" with her husband. "My first affair gave me the reassurance I needed to have the strength to leave my marriage," she wrote.

Her sexual awakening made her a less tense, rigid, and angry person. "Now that I'm thin I enjoy sex more with other people. I'm less inhibited. I have some stretch marks and looseness in the abdomen, but I can now submerge any discomfort in the pleasure I get from my sensuality. Sex is a much, much better experience for me now. I no longer have to masturbate to relieve sexual tension; now I do it because it feels good."

She's still involved with the man she left her husband for, but now that she's single, she also sees another man three times a week and has a number of platonic relationships with male friends. She does not want another exclusive relationship. "The next thirty years promise to be much better than the last thirty have been. I feel free and alive. I'm growing into a woman."

For married women who have lost sexual self-esteem, divorce can provide the chance to rediscover their sexual selves. It is not simply that numbers count, although as we've seen, experience is certainly a factor in sexual development. The major difference, however, can be traced to the quality of a woman's relationships. Many divorced women said that they had married very young, and by the time they reached their thirties, their marriages had become stale and dull. As one woman wrote, "I expected closer, easier, more meaningful communications with my husband. There was never enough money, enough sex, or enough time because we both overcommitted ourselves to our jobs."

The second time around, however, a woman is considerably wiser. Most reported that their lovers were much more sensitive and considerate than their husbands had been. In a positive loving relationship a woman can begin to see herself in a new way—as beautiful, sensual, exciting.

One divorcée summed up the experience succinctly. "It's like a second adolescence," she said enthusiastically, "because the excitement of dating differs so radically from the dullness of my marriage."

Married Sex

In light of these glowing reports from happy divorcées, what do married women have to say about their sex lives? Sadly, over 40 percent of the respondents reported that they still did not enjoy sex and, in most cases, were nonorgasmic.

Maybe I'm a cold tomato, who knows? I really don't think sex is so important to a woman. I haven't had any affairs. I surely don't need any more sex.

A woman married for fourteen years

Some women are born sexy and some are not. I'm just one of those women who doesn't care about sex.

A thirty-three-year-old television executive

Have you ever made love to someone who didn't believe in foreplay or lubricants? It always hurt. I knew I had to leave him from the day we were first married.

I was using the rhythm method and I'd say I was ready and he'd tell me to wait two or three days. We went for three or four months with no sex. I kept going on diets so that he'd want to make love to me. I was as boyish as I could have been, but he

*still didn't want to. After we split up, he moved in
with a homosexual man we'd both known.*

> A thirty-two-year-old cab
> driver

The results of a recent sex survey of over a hundred
thousand women by *Cosmopolitan* magazine, published in
their September 1980 issue, confirm the fact that married
women are less sexually active than their single sisters.
"Daily sex is three times more common among singles with
live-in partners than among married women. And while
fifty percent of the former group make love three to five
times a week, only forty percent of married women have
sex that frequently."

It is tempting to assume, on the basis of these statistics,
that marriage may not always be in a woman's best sexual
interests. But that is not necessarily true. The problem, for
most of these women, is linked to their own sexual indoctrination—their role patterning—and the kind of relationship they have with their husbands. At the most basic level,
these are the women for whom the liberating effects of the
sexual revolution came too late. Despite all recent knowledge about female sexuality, many still believe they are inherently frigid. They simply can't unlearn all those years of
sexual repression and inhibition.

As a group, they tend to be more male-identified than
their more liberated peers, and they continue to view sex
as a way of pleasing their men and fulfilling their role as a
"good" wife. Consequently, they don't believe they are
capable of, or entitled to, pleasure of their own.

The Indentured Homemaker

Laura is a thirty-nine-year-old former Pan American
stewardess, married for fourteen years to a successful busi-

nessman. She and her husband have three children and live in a luxurious city apartment.

Laura still believes that sex is something a man wants, and that, as a good wife, she has to spread her legs and comply. "George thinks I should be more interested in sex than I am. But half the time I'm too tired and I'd rather watch TV. I'd make love once every ten days or less if it were up to me. Maybe once a month! He wants it *constantly,* twice a week at least. I can't get in the mood for sex if we've just had an argument or the kids are running around. He can."

Like many indentured homemakers, she feels bored and restless, yet she does not know what she wants to do with her life. "I think every woman in her thirties goes through a phase of getting tired of staying home, cooking and cleaning, or going out with her girl friends. I miss flying."

Economically dependent on her husband, Laura cannot assert herself, even to say no to sex when he feels like it and she doesn't. As a wife, she doesn't think she has rights. Like many long-married women who have never enjoyed sex, she does *not* blame her husband for being a careless or insensitive lover. Instead, she believes that she is frigid.

"Frigidity," explains Dr. Lila Swell, author of *Success: You Can Make It Happen,* "is really fear of expressing one's sexual being. A woman who has been raised to believe sexual feelings are wrong inhibits or represses those feelings. The sexually assertive woman, on the other hand, has worked out her guilt. She feels free to express herself without punishment or reprisal."

Moreover, women like Laura are still hampered by their own lack of sexual experience. A surprisingly high percentage of women reported that they had never had sex with any man other than their husbands, and consequently, they were totally dependent on their husbands for their sensual fulfillment. And, in many cases, their husbands weren't aware of or willing to provide the kind of foreplay and prolonged lovemaking that women need to achieve orgasms. This, in fact, is a major problem among over-thirty women.

Over-thirty men have internalized the same myths and double standards that women have. Raised to see the sex act as a performance, as a means to their own pleasure and a way of proving their manhood, many American men avoid genuine intimacy. Indeed, "slam bam, thank you ma'am" still seems to be the American way.

My husband was very hot to marry me, but his sex drive evaporated after a few years. Once I came out nude and stood in front of the television set and begged him to make love to me. He just told me to move over so he could watch the Dallas Cowboys.

A thirty-three-year-old divorcée

My husband couldn't find my clitoris during the entire ten years we were married!

A thirty-four-year-old mother of two

Sex has never met my expectations in my marriage.

A thirty-year-old secretary

I enjoy the regularity and availability of sex in my marriage, but I miss the sensual variety of single-hood. Frankly, I enjoy sex less now.

A thirty-two-year-old professional woman

Sexually, my marriage is not what I expected it to be. I had always anticipated we would be ideal, with simultaneous orgasms and all, but it hasn't worked out that way. My husband just isn't very interested in sex.

A thirty-five-year-old
midwesterner

According to Dr. Witkin, "Many men as well as women still don't know that the clitoris, and not the vagina, is the center of the female's erotic response. Many men also don't know that it takes a female much longer to have an orgasm than a man. A man can get excited and have an orgasm in five minutes. A woman usually needs about twenty minutes to an hour of stimulation before she can have an orgasm.

"Also, too many men are penis-oriented. A man can learn to give a woman orgasms all day if he wants to by using his tongue and his hands."

But many men are threatened by the notion that the penis is not the sole, or necessarily the best, way to pleasure a woman. The penis is a symbol of their own sense of self, of power and masculinity, and it is very difficult for them to deal with a woman who makes her own sexual demands.

Thus, even if a woman tries to take the initiative and become more experimental, she may find her husband completely uncooperative. "In many marriages," says Dr. Witkin, "the woman becomes more sexual in her thirties and her husband is confused and intimidated. He hasn't been taught that females have a sex drive, and he may think there is something wrong with his wife. He wonders: 'What happened to the docile woman I married. When she was younger, she was only interested in sex when *I* was interested. Now she's the one who wants sex more than I do.' This frightens some men. They can't handle the situation because they've never been taught how to deal with it."

Children can also put a damper on the married woman's sex life. "I hate to have intercourse," one anxious mother wrote, "because I'm worried that my five-year-old will hear us and start asking questions I don't want to have to answer."

Our society does not encourage sexual expression in mothers, and men and women respond to this unconscious stricture in varying ways. Women tend to feel uncomfortable about making love unless the bedroom door is locked and the kids are asleep or away from home. For men the response may be more complex. Once their wives become mothers, they may associate them with their own mothers, and the incest taboo can have an unconscious effect. And if a woman has a strong attachment to her children, her husband may feel left out, unloved, and less interested in sex.

"One of the married couples' biggest problems," says Dr. Witkin, "is that they feel guilty about pleasure. They are troubled by childhood strictures against erotic pleasure. A couple often forgets that it was pleasure in each other that brought them together now that they are immersed in day-to-day problems, money worries, and bringing up children."

What then can the married woman do to improve the quality of her sex life?

Judging by the responses of happily married women, the first important step is communication. Talk honestly with your husband; tell him your feelings and encourage him to talk about his. Avoid accusations and blame. Instead, make a commitment together to become more open and honest in your sexual relationship. Learn what pleases you, learn about your body, and tell your husband what you want and don't want. Set aside time to spend alone together, without the children, to renew your feelings for each other.

One woman said that she and her husband had a baby-sitter who took the children to the park on Saturday afternoons while she and her husband went to bed. She reported that she and her husband now look forward eagerly to these afternoon interludes, and their greater sexual intimacy has spilled over into other aspects of their lives. They argue less, show affection more openly now, which she believes is good for the children, and they even make love more often during the week than they ever did before.

The important point to remember is that you are entitled to pleasure. However, it is equally important to realize that ingrained attitudes don't die an easy death. One unfortunate effect of the sexual revolution is that many women now feel even more inadequae because they think they aren't having the fabulous sex lives all other women are experiencing. This kind of performance pressure creates an added burden of guilt.

"It isn't easy to drop old attitudes overnight," says Sanford Jason. "A woman has to change her feelings, which are harder to change than her intellectual outlook. What we see today among women in their thirties is not sexual revolution but slow sexual evolution."

The women in this study who reported the greatest degree of sexual satisfaction were not necessarily the women who had sex most frequently or who always experienced orgasm. Rather, they were the ones who had accepted their sexuality *on their own terms*. In other words, the issue is not whether you have sex once a week or twice a day or even whether you always reach orgasm but, rather, how *you* feel about your sex life. If you and your husband are satisfied with a passionate encounter once a week, there's no reason to feel impelled to make love more often.

The Extramarital Affair

Women who need more emotional and/or sexual satisfaction than their marriages can provide may opt for an extramarital affair. According to our statistics, 25 percent of women have their first extramarital affair in their thirties. This surprisingly high figure can be linked to the higher sex drive of the over-thirty woman, her continued disappointment with her marriage, and the fact that she wants acknowledgment of her womanliness before she feels she will be too old to attract a man.

However, extramarital affairs are not easy to handle. Some women reported they had experimented with open marriage, only to find that it didn't work or that their marriages broke up as a result.

> *My husband and I agreed to an open marriage, so I had a brief affair with a colleague at a professional convention. I told my husband about it, and he was angry and jealous. I feel guilty for having slept with another man.*
>
> A thirty-three-year-old
> professor

Other women—especially those raised in a strict or religious environment—found that, even though they wanted to, they could not overcome the guilt they felt for violating their moral code.

> *I've been married for fourteen years. My husband resents my job, we can't communicate, and we're always fighting. Our marriage is too confining, and not the least romantic. But it's good for me because it keeps me in line. I spent one night with another*

man, but I felt dirty. I am constantly fighting the
evil temptation to walk on the wild side. Every
day I pray I will stay straight.

A thirty-six-year-old Catholic
from North Carolina

Other women do not have affairs—even though they
might like to—because they know themselves well enough
to realize that a passionate affair would probably end their
marriages. And they may be right. A high percentage of
women who rated their marriages as loveless reported that
they'd left their husbands shortly after becoming involved
with another man. The fact is, despite our much-vaunted
sexual freedom, most of us are not yet very adept at handling casual sex. Perhaps we never will be. And we tend
to fall in love with the men with whom we sleep.

A thirty-eight-year-old professor told me that when she
was thirty-three, she had an affair and fell madly in love. "I
used to tell myself that all this talk about love and passion
was just a fantasy," she said. "I always told myself that I had
two children and a husband who didn't abuse me and that I
should be happy. However, once I had the affair, I realized
that passion does exist. Knowing that, I couldn't not have
it. If my husband had been either my friend or my lover, I
would have stayed in the marriage. But he was neither and
I had to leave."

She and her husband divorced, but her affair ended because the man was unwilling to make a commitment. "That
was my worst year," she said. "I thought I'd developed
breast cancer, and I had to get a job. However, I had some
good friends who helped me get through the transition. I
endured."

She joined an organization called Parents Without
Partners, and she met her second husband at a meeting. He

had also been married before—to a woman who didn't love him. He had been searching for passion, "a D. H. Lawrence transcendent sexual relationship," and they found what they were looking for in each other.

"Love exists," she told me. "That's what I've learned. And sex for us is an important and crucial part of that love. We had both been denied sex all our lives, and for us it was like finding water on a desert. We are passionate lovers as well as best friends."

Although many women fantasize about a truly passionate relationship, most are unwilling to walk away from their marriages, even if they are involved with other men. Obviously, children and financial concerns have a great deal to do with their reluctance to start over. Moreover, many women, especially those who fear being alone, are so uncertain about finding a new partner that they can't or won't leave what security they do have, even if it's in the form of a boring marriage. But these women do pay a price. Over and over I heard women complain bitterly about the lack of sharing, romance, and passion in their lackluster marriages.

> *I try to be a good wife and mother, but I wish I'd never married. My husband and I share less than we did ten years ago. I began an affair at thirty-one with a former boss. We are extremely close and best of friends. Once my children are older, I hope I can leave my marriage. I will die if I have to stay married to my husband for the rest of my life.*

> A thirty-two-year-old mother from Nebraska

> *My husband and I share less than we used to. I have had one satisfying affair that lasted two years. We are desperately good friends and enduring*

*lovers. I could live without him, but I don't want
to. I will never forget him or regret the relationship. It has made my life richer.*

> A thirty-four-year-old woman
> from North Dakota with three
> children

Although there were major differences in the way
women conduct and cope with affairs, one common motiva-
tional thread did emerge. The over-thirty woman turns to
other men in a desperate attempt to find appreciation and
acknowledgment of her worth as a woman. She wants to
feel emotionally alive and appreciated on a sexual/emo-
tional level.

Returning to the work force can be a catalyst for an
affair of this kind. A woman discovers that there are men
who find her attractive, flirt with her, appreciate her. If her
husband has ignored her or taken her for granted, she may
have an affair as a way of reaffirming her desirability.

"Extramarital affairs," explains sexual therapist Virginia Johnson, "are a symptom of a woman's deeper need to
learn who she is—not just a wife or mother but, in her own
terms, the total person she feels capable of becoming."

Why do women seek self-esteem in a lover's arms? Ba-
sically, because that's what we were taught to do. From infancy on, we learned to seek our own identity via men. If
we were popular, if men wanted us, we'd succeeded as
women. We saw our own desirability, our very worth as individuals, only in terms of how men saw us. Is it any wonder, therefore, that many of us can't break out of that trap?
At the very same time that we were learning to deny our
sexual nature, we were also learning that our sexuality was
what made us lovable, kissable, huggable. This confusing
dual message—to emphasize our bodies and charms to at-

tract men while saying no to the very desire we'd struggled to spark—is what really accounts for the confusion we see among so many women in their thirties.

Self-esteem develops from the inside out. If a woman turns to an affair as a way to validate her identity, she'll only plummet back to earth when the affair ends. The best marriages and relationships, as we've seen, are those where both partners have a firm sense of self. We cannot expect anyone else to give us that sense; we have to do it ourselves.

Affairs are probably destructive if a woman views them as the only way to provide excitement or bring her a measure of self-esteem. And if she feels degraded or exploited or is anxious or unhappy as a result, the affair can actually lower what self-esteem she has. A woman who does not end a relationship that has sadistic undertones must work on building up her storehouse of self-love in order to overcome morbid dependency on men.

However, if a woman has grounded feelings of identity, she may approach an affair as a way to get in touch with her sexuality. Pleasure without emotional involvement is still a new idea for many women, although men have practiced it for years.

A thirty-five-year-old Beverly Hills homemaker wrote in to say that she had *expected* to have a more passionate relationship with her husband, "to be loved mightily in a way that seems impossible in this marriage." Although she lives "in the world's most beautiful home" and has "everything material I could possibly want," she is becoming more and more estranged from her husband. She experienced "creeping loneliness" the Christmas she was thirty-three, because of the lack of talking, sharing, or lovemaking in her relationship.

As a result, she embarked on "two short-lived affairs" and said she "enjoyed every minute of both. I didn't feel guilty," she wrote. "I found it much easier to wildly love someone I had no responsibility for, and I found my husband more attractive afterward. The women's movement has made me much more appreciative of my sexuality, my capacity has increased dramatically, and my need for physical loving is far greater than I ever knew. *It is quite possible that occasional encounters with other men will be what keeps me sane."*

Celibacy—A New Option

One of the most interesting findings to emerge from this study is that more and more unmarried women of this generation—whether single, widowed, or divorced—are choosing to remain celibate, if not forever, at least for long periods of time. When one considers the broad array of sexual options possible today and the freedom we have to pursue them, this finding takes on even greater significance. Why are so many over-thirty women making such a choice?

Although individual motivations vary, one common theme runs through most of the comment I heard. The fact is that many women feel the price they pay for sex is too high in terms of emotional disappointment and psychological pain.

> *I see men as a necessary evil. I approach them with care, and I am no longer disappointed when nothing materializes. I prefer being alone.*

> A thirty-two-year-old woman
> divorced twice

> *I see no one much of the time because I'd rather be alone than in a relationship that isn't a quality one.*

> A thirty-four-year-old divorcée

> *I've been celibate since I turned thirty because I*
> *want a relationship with someone who gives me*
> *more than physical satisfaction.*

A thirty-one-year-old woman

These women are the casualties of the sexual revolution. Although one can argue that the sexual revolution has helped women, permitting us to express our sexuality without guilt, it is equally true that the emphasis on casual sex, without benefit of commitment or genuine intimacy, has made many women feel exploited and used. It is ironic that in gaining the freedom to say yes, we've lost the freedom to say no.

In the early seventies, when casual guilt-free sex became an option for women for the first time in history, it appeared to many to be a marvelous new freedom. At long last women could revel in their sexuality in the same way that men always had, pursuing pleasure for the sake of pleasure. And in that first flush of excitement, we thought we'd found the answer to many of the problems that had plagued men and women for centuries. By accepting sex as a natural part of daily existence, a necessary physical function like eating, sleeping, or breathing, we'd banished all those expectations, fears, and myths that had divided men and women for so long. But for many of us, the reality simply didn't live up to this utopian vision. Casual sex—whether in the form of a brief affair or a one-night stand—was lonely, painful, and profoundly dissatisfying.

> *Like Janis Joplin, my heroine, I was going to be*
> *"free." But I look back at my life now and I'm*
> *angry. I feel I was used and exploited by men. I was*
> *a receptacle for them. I feel I made the wrong*
> *choices. I wish I had settled on family and babies.*

At least now I would have something to show for all the love, care, and support I gave men.

> A thirty-five-year-old
> Manhattanite

I don't know why people keep writing and writing about orgasms. It's easy for a man to give a woman orgasms. I've been having them since I was five years old. What's hard to find is a man willing to give a woman love.

> A thirty-three-year-old
> administrative assistant with
> too many married men in
> her life

The term *casual sex* is rather a misnomer because there is nothing very casual about sex. Sex, by its very nature, is an intimate encounter. You shed your clothes and allow yourself to become vulnerable. We humans, moreover, are sensitive, fragile creatures. We thrive on love, stability, and acceptance. Since women seem to be more in touch with their emotions than men, they are often quicker to acknowledge this need for intimacy.

While many men have been raised to see sex as a form of conquest, we women see it as the highest expression of love. And it's difficult for many of us to abandon these ideas. Whether so many women are turned off to the idea of casual sex because we were raised in a repressive atmosphere or because we are inherently monogamous and more needy of affection than men is certainly arguable. But the fact remains that thousands of unmarried over-thirty women are shying away from these encounters, choosing solitude in preference to having a man whom they don't care about warming their bed for a night. As one woman told me, "I can't separate sex from feelings for another person." Another wrote, "I tried casual sex, but it seemed hollow to me —a waste of time. I can have orgasms by myself and at least I don't run the risk of getting pregnant or catching venereal disease."

The result is that large numbers of women are simply not interested in expressing their sexuality, except within the confines of committed relationships. And for them, celibacy is the only possible choice between such relationships.

> *I find it difficult to have a sexual relationship with someone I do not feel close to. I tend to conduct myself in a monogamous fashion, even though I live alone. Lacking a steady partner at some periods of my recent life, I find I become celibate until a very strong attraction comes along, which nearly always leads to my next serious affair.*
>
> A thirty-four-year-old disc jockey

> *In my twenties I didn't have to be in love to have a lover. All I needed was someone I was highly attracted to. Now I'm less interested in sex in a purely physical sense, and value real communion between souls. My lover has to share certain values, such as honesty and sincerity. I can't waste time anymore on frivolous lovers. This is my life here and now. Up until the time I turned thirty, it was a rehearsal.*
>
> A thirty-six year-old archaeologist

Many women become celibate because they are so profoundly disillusioned with men and the quality of sharing possible in many "modern" relationships. As one thirty-five-year-old woman whose husband left her for another woman told me, "I distrust men and have none in my life. I'll never be any man's slave again, and all of the men I've met demand it to some degree."

These women are angry and feel—perhaps rightly— that they've been victimized by the new sexual mores. If they say no, a man may turn his attention elsewhere. If they say yes, the man may disappear from their lives the next morning. For the fact is that while most men pay lip service to the idea of female sexual equality, many continue to believe that a sexually free woman is somehow "not nice."

For other men the sexual revolution has become a legitimate route to fulfilling their fantasy lives. Lured on by the *Playboy* image of the swinging single, married men are leaving their wives to pursue their own vision of sexual freedom. And others, shunning such "antiquated values" as monogamy and commitment, are pursuing affairs with vigor, while their wives pick up the pieces.

When I was thirty-one, my husband and I separated. He wanted to have sex with many ladies, and I wanted a monogamous relationship. I was too jealous to compromise. During our breakup, I was depressed and frightened, and there was a lot of sadness. I underwent surgery. I had the feeling that life was unfair, and that I didn't deserve it to be so bad.

A thirty-seven-year-old
kindergarten teacher and
Quaker

My husband had an affair with my sister. It broke my heart. Yet I was still consumed with guilt because I believed a good mother doesn't ask the

*father to leave. It was hard for me to accept the fact
that we should divorce.*

A thirty-three-year-old
paraprofessional teacher

*My husband just told me I'm getting too old, and
he wants his freedom. I have two twins, six years
old! Part of me still refuses to believe that life is
working out like this. The houselights are going to
go on, the curtain will go down, and someone is
going to say, okay, the play is over now. This has
been a test. You have passed and your marriage will
be happy.*

A thirty-eight-year-old
California resident

*I consider leaving my husband every time I find out
about one of his affairs. He always picks these dainty,
very dependent women, next to whom I feel fat and
ugly. However, I can't imagine living alone. My
body isn't a ten anymore.*

A thirty-seven-year-old mother
of three

"By the time a man reaches his late thirties or early
forties," says Dr. Gerald Bernstein, a Manhattan internist,
"he is feeling pretty good about himself. He's advanced in
his career. He looks in the mirror and says to himself, 'God
I'm great.' Then he looks at his over-thirty wife, and she's
the mommy. Maybe she's gained weight. He feels she's got-
ten stale. He says to himself, 'I have to spread my wings.' In
his midlife crisis, he wants to experience sexual emancipa-
tion and date younger women."

In the past, the man who abandoned his wife and children would have been considered deplorable. Today, however, especially as a result of the collapse of the extended family, many men feel less and less pressure to honor commitments.

"If you read *Penthouse* magazine," says divorce lawyer Sidney Friedler, "or any other pornographic men's magazine, you will see that they portray a highly unrealistic picture of marriage. According to their scenario, the man is supposed to come home to be greeted by his wife, who is wearing a black negligee. Sometimes, they have fantastic sex on the living room floor. Or, after dinner, they go to the neighbors to engage in wife swapping and have oral sex.

"In real life, the man goes home to his wife who is grappling with her own disappointments, fantasies, and resentments. And he may feel disappointed and cheated sexually.

"So, to find the sex he wants, he may begin to have affairs or ask for an open marriage. Since these choices don't usually work out, the couple may end up getting a divorce."

Another group of women reported that sex simply wasn't very important to them.

> *Sex is much less important to me than it was in my twenties, and I have it less often. I masturbate and have orgasms by myself. I still believe that women are better at doing it for themselves than men are at trying to do it for them. I find masturbation perfectly normal and healthy and don't think people should feel guilty about it. Our society does sex a lot of harm by cheapening it and being obsessed with it.*
>
> A thirty-six-year-old woman

A high-powered corporate executive vice-president told me that she and her husband rarely make love. Her work provides enough fulfillment, and she's consciously chosen to devote her time and energy to that aspect of her life. Nor is she interested in extramarital affairs. "I have a hard enough time in my office getting men to respect me and take me seriously. I often travel with five or six colleagues, but the issue of sex just never comes up."

For women like this, says Dr. Helen Singer Kaplan, associate clinical professor of psychiatry at New York Hospital Cornell Medical Center, celibacy is a healthy choice. "For some people, sex is fraught with so much anxiety, and negative emotion, that it may be a better adaptation not to risk it."

In fact, periods of celibacy can be healthy and emotionally necessary for many women. It is a time to refuel, to get in touch with yourself and your goals, to put your energy into new projects. The knowledge that you are capable of going it alone, of relying solely on yourself, can be an invaluable way of building self-esteem.

One thirty-seven-year-old woman wrote in to say that she noticed she had developed a pattern of taking on a new project after each of her two love affairs had ended. For her this was an integral part of the healing process. At thirty-two she bought a house and renovated it. At thirty-five, when her second affair ended, she "got three pets and stopped seeing men." She also took up organic gardening. When I heard from her, she'd just started seeing men again but would not sleep with them unless it seemed likely that an emotional involvement would develop. In "returning" to the 1950s rules about sex—holding out for a special man— this woman found a way to deal with the new problems we're facing in this era of casual sex and equally casual relationships.

* * *

As we move into the 1980s, we must begin to ask ourselves some hard questions about sex. Although few of us want to see a return of the repressive attitudes of the 1950s, it is to be hoped that the lessons we've learned in the "swinging seventies" will enable us to pioneer new, healthy ways of relating to men. If we commit ourselves to expressing our sexuality within honest, committed, caring relationships, perhaps we will realize that utopian vision we thought we'd found earlier.

CHAPTER
6

The Lesbian Experience

In the 1950s I had never heard the word *lesbian*. Like the noun *oncidium*, it was not part of my vocabulary. Our "good girl" training did not acknowledge that women could be attracted to other women.

However, our values and beliefs have undergone great changes in the last fifteen years, and homosexuality has finally come out of the closet. The gay rights movement has been actively promulgating the idea that homosexuality is simply another sexual choice, neither right nor wrong, simply different.

This has had a profound effect on our generation of women. One of the most astonishing findings to emerge from this study was the significantly large number of women who were taking their first female lovers in their thirties. In fact, many were ending heterosexual marriages in order to pursue homosexual life-styles. At first, it was hard to believe that in the heartland of America, women were exchanging penises for vaginas. However, there is an underground revolution going on, one with vast implications for changes in the structure of our society.

Coming Out I: Dorothy

Dorothy Ray (a pseudonym) is a middle-class Jewish woman who attended a Long Island high school near mine. Her father is an internist; her mother, a suburban home-maker. In school Dorothy was widely respected: a brilliant if reserved, always immaculately dressed, student. She married her high school sweetheart and adopted a suburban life-style like her mother's. Her husband opened a small store, and Dorothy cheerfully began raising two cherished daughters.

We had our first reunion in many years while I was writing this book. Dorothy looked almost exactly as I had remembered her. She even wore the same hairstyle she'd had fifteen years before. She was still pencil-thin and beautifully dressed. She had hardly aged at all.

She said she'd been studying photography for the last three years and had set up a studio in the basement of her home. She found it an important creative outlet, a means to get in touch with who she was, how she looked at life, what was meaningful to her. Instead of spending hours discussing the personal intrigues of bored housebound neighbors, she discussed the techniques of W. Eugene Smith, Bea Nettles, and Diane Arbus with passionate colleagues. It was a different world . . . of art and wonder, competition and beauty. To Dorothy, who had plunged into it with the desperation of a drowning woman, it was salvation.

The second time we met Dorothy announced, "Jim and I are getting a divorce." She described her husband as uninteresting, unappealing, and joyless. "He's actually a little strange. He doesn't talk very much. It's difficult to get him to discuss his feelings about anything. . . ." For years, she had catered to him, devoting all her time to meeting his needs and expectations. She had been a model wife and mother. In addition to her domestic duties, she had done the bookkeeping for his business, and when Jim wanted to open a second store, her father had given them ten thousand dollars.

However, as she changed and grew through her passionate involvement with photography, she became more and more uncomfortable with Jim. Her warmth and creativity were at odds with his distant, rather cold personality. There were frequent conflicts. Now, divorce seemed to be the only solution.

A week later I heard from Dorothy's best friend. "I had to call someone," Karen said. "You're the only person I could think of who would understand." She sounded disturbed and out of breath. "There's another reason why Dorothy wants to break up with Jim. She has a woman lover!"

"Dorothy is a lesbian?"

"I can hardly believe it," Karen said. "Dorothy has been my best friend since we were four years old. My best friend! And I never had the slightest idea. . . ." She paused. "I don't dare tell my husband. If he knew, he would never let me see her again."

"How is she?"

"Everything is terrible. That's why I found out. She *had* to tell someone. It seems that she confessed to Jim that she was in love with Marge, a woman she's been seeing for the last three years. That was on Wednesday. By Thursday he had told his parents, his parents had told her parents, and everyone was thoroughly horrified and shocked. His parents are pressing him to fight for custody of the children on the grounds that she is an unfit mother. After all these years!

"Dorothy is extremely upset." Karen's voice trailed off, as if she couldn't find the words to express what she wanted to say. "It's so *unnatural!* I mean, you can understand a man and woman having sex. At least we produce children! But two women?"

Why Women Turn to Women

How can we understand a suburban housewife and mother falling in love with a woman in the fourth decade of her life? How can we account for the many other women I heard from, who are amazingly, unaccountably, having homosexual affairs in their thirties?

> *I was a housewife pulling up crabgrass in the early 1960s. Two years ago I divorced and met the person of my dreams—a woman! Jan and I are in love and hope to live together the rest of our lives.*
>
> A thirty-eight-year-old teacher

> *I've had fantasies about women for a few years, but when I was thirty-two, I had my first affair with a woman. It was the most beautiful experience of my life. I still feel a little guilty because my church doesn't support my choice. However, this is the best thing that ever happened to me, and I can't walk away.*
>
> A thirty-four-year-old
> Cleveland Catholic

> *In my twenties I had no idea I was a lesbian.*
>
> A thirty-five-year-old divorced
> therapist

> *I was divorced at thirty after two years of marriage. My ex-husband and I thought I was bisexual, but it turns out that I'm gay.*
>
> A thirty-three-year-old black
> affirmative action officer

Many of the women I heard from had married in their early twenties, expecting, as so many of us did, to live happily ever after. When disillusionment sets in, many blame themselves at first and spend several years trying to work things out with their husbands. But as they approach that deadline decade, they become impatient; they're no longer willing to waste time fighting what seems to be a losing battle for happiness. A new sense of urgency impels them to make new choices, especially at a time when most women are becoming less inhibited, more assertive, and more sexual.

We can pinpoint five reasons why women in their thirties take women as lovers:

• Two women have the opportunity to transcend the traditional male-female roles that so often get in the way of genuine and spontaneous relationships.

• Women who have been emotionally deprived in their relationships with men revel in the quality of sharing possible between two women.

• Women who have found little pleasure in sex attain unprecedented levels of excitement and satisfaction with a female lover. Many report having had their first orgasms in the arms of another woman.

• Women who have always defined themselves through men—as someone's wife, daughter, or mother—find tremendous satisfaction in taking charge of their own lives. Most report that their newfound independence leads to a dramatic increase in self-esteem and confidence.

• Women who were gay, or who were aware of an attraction for other women, married men instead, conforming to the rigid social codes of the 1950s. Now they are seeing a more receptive climate and taking a risk, leaving marriages that were not fulfilling to begin with. Many of them retain friendships with their husbands.

* * *

As yet there is no consensus about the "causes" of homosexuality. Some scientists have theorized that it is a genetic trait; others believe that it is a choice based on myriad psychological factors in childhood and adolescence. "This issue has been batted around for years," says Dr. Barbara Sang, a clinical psychiatrist practicing in New York, "but no one knows the answer. All they know is that lesbian women, unlike their male counterparts, have no problem making a commitment."

In *Homosexualities: A Study of Human Diversity Among Men and Women,* authors Alan P. Bell and Martin S. Weinberg report that 38 percent of the lesbian women they interviewed were monogamous within committed relationships, happy, and well adjusted. Others were more sexually active but well adjusted too. Only 8 percent of the women were poorly adjusted and/or in psychotherapy.

The authors concluded that "the homosexual females did not differ from the heterosexual females in many measures of psychological adjustment. . . . Many homosexuals could very well serve as models of social comportment and psychological maturity. Most are indistinguishable from the heterosexual majority with respect to most of the nonsexual aspects of their lives." Moreover, the majority of homosexual women reported that "they did not at all regret being homosexual, had never seriously considered discontinuing their homosexuality, did not think of it as an emotional disorder, and would not mind if a child of theirs became homosexual."

In short, contrary to prevalent myths, lesbians are *psychologically healthy.*

Coming Out II: Jennifer's First Experience

Jennifer was born to an Episcopalian family in Atlanta, Georgia. In her early twenties she married a man she was "madly in love with." She became a teacher to help put him through medical school and continued to help out financially even after she gave birth to a son. During those early years of marriage she described herself as "the perfect wife" or "superwife."

"I would cook things like fresh trout stuffed with salmon and dill with a pastry crust wrapped around it. Every night he got a gourmet meal. And that was on top of nursing my son, working, and doing the housework."

Even though she earned a paycheck, her husband was the boss. "I wasn't even allowed to go to the movies by myself."

Like many women who eventually choose homosexuality, her sex life was disastrous. "I felt like a bagel. I was just a hole. My husband didn't allow me to move or make any noise. He never kissed me or showed me any tenderness. I felt very frustrated. I wanted to feel loved and cherished."

The reason she didn't have orgasms, her husband said, was that she was frigid. "If I ever complained even the tiniest bit or tried to be assertive about acting out any of my fantasies, I was told that I was undermining his masculinity."

A few years after her husband had established a medical practice, he asked for a divorce. "When he left, I was beside myself. My whole world crumbled. I was pretty desperate, and since I couldn't find a teaching job, I took a job as an executive secretary. I became involved with several younger men. However, my feelings about men were slowly changing. I kept being disappointed. The relationships were unsatisfying. The only positive thing that happened to me during this time was that, after reading a few books, I learned to masturbate to orgasm. And I stopped feeling guilty about it."

She found herself becoming closer and closer to one

woman friend. "I was very attracted to her. A few years ago I would have been horrified, but I had been reading the diaries of Anaïs Nin, who had an affair with a woman, and that relieved some of my misgivings.

"One day, at her house, I told her I loved her and wanted to sleep with her. To my relief she said, 'I've been thinking the same thing.' It was the first time anyone had kissed me in about five years. It was scary and it was sweet. Neither of us knew what we were doing, and yet both of us knew what we were doing!"

The affair lasted only three days. "Neither of us could handle it. I slept with a man right after that, to prove to myself I was straight. The realization that I was turned on by women was horrifying. I thought, but I'm not one of them! I don't seduce little girls. I don't wear oversized men's shirts. So I had an affair with a man to prove that I was still a woman."

After two more disappointing relationships with men, she began to frequent some gay bars in Manhattan.

"The first time I went in alone, I was frightened to death. I was shy and wouldn't dance. But everybody was having such a good time and the women were so free that I began to feel more and more comfortable."

She met an older woman and began a second affair. "My feelings about her are very intense. I'm in love with her. In the beginning I needed her so much I would have done anything to keep her."

The relationship has lasted six months. "I am calmer," Jennifer reports, "but I'll be devastated if the relationship breaks up."

She and her lover do not live together; they maintain separate apartments. Their social life revolves around a group of gay women, with whom they attend parties and cultural events. "I like the idea that I've made all these new friends. We all have careers and a lot in common. I was always bored with my husband's business friends, and yet they were my social circle."

Jennifer says that her sexual choice has increased, rather than detracted from, her feelings of womanliness. "I'm more conscious of, and at ease with, my appearance. I had to get into other women to find out about me. Women are wonderful. I'm aware now that I'm an attractive woman and I feel more attractive. If anything, I've become more consciously feminine. I'm more vain than I ever was. Before, I never thought of myself as anything but a plain, undesirable failure."

In contrast to many women who keep this part of their lives secret, Jennifer chose to be open about her relationship. "It's not a good example to my child if I live a lie. I'm not guilty about my choice. If I lose my integrity, what else do I have?" But this decision has had unpleasant consequences. "I've lost a lot of female friends who couldn't deal with my changes, but the really valuable friends are still there. My mother doesn't speak to me, and my father is very unhappy about my choice."

Her ex-husband also hit the roof. "He called me a filthy stinking dyke pervert lesbian pig. Originally, we were going to have an amicable divorce, but now he is fighting for custody of our child on the grounds that I am gay. The custody case is his vendetta for not being able to control my life anymore.

"One night he broke into my apartment and raped me. He is not paying court-ordered child support. I had to rush my son to Philadelphia to keep him from being kidnapped."

Jennifer's story raises some important points about the choice of lesbianism.

Perhaps the most revealing—and surprising—was that, like other women I've heard from, she does not regret or feel ashamed of her new involvement with women. Indeed, she feels strengthened. Many women reported that their homosexual relationships helped to cure the depression that had plagued them for years. In the arms of another woman, they found that they could respect themselves in a way that hadn't been possible with men.

> *I'm more comfortable with my body and dress with more individuality now. I have no more depression.*
>
> A thirty-three-year-old ex-housewife now studying psychology

> *Ever since I've become involved with women, my self-esteem has skyrocketed. I know that sounds crazy. Maybe you don't even believe me. But it's true. I think I always had fantasies that other women were different from me—that they were more confident, smarter, smelled better.*
>
> *Now I've learned other women are just like me. I'm not as compulsively competitive with women as I was when I was seeing men. My relationships are less destructive, and I'm happier. I have found that there is much less game playing involved in a relationship with a woman, and that makes me more secure. I'm having more fun now than I ever had.*
>
> A thirty-six-year-old ex-tennis champ

Naturally, psychological liberation is not immediate or guaranteed. Jennifer's initial ambivalence about making love with a woman is a common theme. The choice defies all the expectations she had about herself as a woman. The negative attitudes we all learned about lesbians cause many women to react with fear and shame. They wonder if they are "queers" or "freaks." Women who are unable to resolve these feelings often repress their sexuality or remain so guilt-ridden that they avoid sex with either men or women. Moreover, not every first or second homosexual experience is a positive one. One thirty-eight-year-old adventurous heterosexual told me she had slept with a woman simply because she was curious. They were not close friends or even passionately attracted to each other. Perhaps predictably, the experience for her was "just as disappointing as having casual sex with a man." No bells rang, the earth didn't shake, and she did not care to repeat the experience.

On the other hand, a positive relationship with a woman can radically change a woman's feelings about herself, sometimes precipitating a major change in life-style.

A Political Choice

When we define the lesbian woman only in terms of her sexuality, we minimize the complexity of her personality. Barbara Ponse, in her book *Identities in the Lesbian World: The Social Construction of Self,* explains it this way. "Within the lesbian world, the source of essentiality moves beyond sexuality, implying an expansion of the experience of self and a finding of community. Lesbian sexuality is seen as an emanation from the essential self; lesbianism is a totality of which sexuality is a mere part."

In other words, the homosexual woman chooses to spend her time with women rather than with men. She may feel more comfortable around women, enjoys their company more. She may feel she has little in common with most men, that she has to put on a false face with men, trying to fit a stereotypical idea of femininity that does not feel natural to her.

This can be especially true in the case of an assertive,

powerful woman who has had men react with fear or hostility to the strength of her personality.

> *I simply got tired of having to conform to what men
> expected of me. I tend to be loud and boisterous,
> and I love to tell jokes. However, most of the men
> I've dated feel threatened by my behavior, so I
> would have to tone myself down or risk being
> thought of as unfeminine.*
>
> *However, around women, I can let my hair
> down and just be myself. I don't have to conform
> to anyone's expectations, except my own.*

A thirty-four-year-old musician

> *The first woman's dance I attended was a real eye-
> opener for me. There were over three hundred
> women—all shapes, sizes, and colors—having an
> absolute ball. It wasn't like the disco scene, when
> the women are focused on whether they are going
> to be chosen by a man to dance.*
>
> *There were tremendous feelings of friendship
> among the women. Nobody was competing. It was
> the first time I really understood that women were
> okay people, and that we didn't need men to make
> us feel good about ourselves. We could give that
> love to each other. This didn't mean that I had to
> sleep with a woman. It meant that it was great to
> be a woman, that women were just as terrific and
> interesting as men.*

A thirty-one-year-old bank
teller

When women become close to women—something that
has only occurred on a large scale in the last fifteen years—

feelings of closeness and warmth develop. For some women sex seems like the logical next step in forming a bond of intimacy. For this reason a significant number of women (although by no means a majority, as some antifeminists might argue) who have become feminists often make the political-emotional-sexual choice of lesbianism.

Once a woman becomes a feminist, she starts to value herself more as a woman—to take her rights seriously. We say that she becomes woman-identified, that is, she feels entitled to the same pleasures and privileges men have always had.

As she becomes more committed, she becomes more conscious of herself as a female and of her bonds with other women. For some feminists it feels odd to exert three-quarters of their energy on women's issues and at the same time have a relationship with a man who is not at all interested in "the cause."

Transcending Roles

In fact, for many women the traditional definition of femininity has been a major factor in their choice of a homosexual life-style. Women report that they have found it extremely difficult to overcome traditional male-female roles in relationships with men. With a woman a different dynamic can occur.

> *I got tired of asking my husband to help me clear off the table, to help me do the shopping and cleaning when the holidays came, tired of having to pick up his socks and serve him his meals. Now I'm living with a woman, and the relationship is a thousand times easier. There are no roles. She doesn't play the man and I don't play the woman. We are role-free. For the first time I am in a relationship in*

*which both our needs, and interests, are considered
equally important.*

A thirty-four-year-old
marketing assistant

*When I was in my twenties, my goals were to be the
wife of a successful man, admired and desired by
men and envied by women. By thirty I was angry,
frustrated, and bored. My husband and I divorced
when I was thirty-three.*

*I fell in love with a twenty-two-year-old man
but felt insecure and confused. I spent the next year
on a kibbutz. At thirty-five I moved from Chicago
to Seattle, worked as a railroad brakeperson, and
lived with an alcoholic for six miserable months.*

*I turned thirty-six in frustration, anger, and
confusion. However, the past year has been one of
self-acceptance. I fell in love with a woman and
began to define myself as a lesbian. I'm a beautiful,
powerful, loving woman, which is a world away
from being somebody's wife. I don't want to be
owned by anyone else. Having a relationship with
a man is just too difficult. Men want servants, not
equal relationships.*

A thirty-seven-year-old member
of a collective bakery in Seattle

For women who have been locked into a subservient
or dependent position in their marriages, the role freedom
possible in lesbian relationships is an important factor in
the alleviation of depression we see in our sample.

Although women who take their first female lovers in
their thirties often do so because their relationships with
men have been unsatisfactory or disappointing, this does

not mean that all over-thirty lesbians are on the rebound from men. Many are thoroughly dissatisfied with men and never approach a woman; others have experienced great satisfaction with individual men but, unaccountably, prefer women. The point is that her disappointment with heterosexual relationships is a frequent, and often conscious, component of a woman's choice of female lovers. The following story involves both of these dynamics.

The Disappointed Princess

Theresa, a tall, beautiful thirty-four-year-old woman with two children, was married at nineteen. She was a virgin. As the years passed, the love she and her husband had felt for each other was slowly replaced by disappointment and hostility. He was jealous of their two children and resented the time and attention Theresa gave them. Three times he hit her while she was pregnant. The marriage became a place for each of them to act out their anger toward the other. He threw tantrums and she withdrew.

During their last year of marriage, she noticed that she became excited every time she planned to visit a certain woman friend. "I loved everything about her—her intelligence, warmth, and vivacity, but I never told her the way I felt and our relationship never progressed beyond friendship."

Several months later Theresa was divorced. She moved to California and met a woman fifteen years her senior, who had had six children while she was married but who was now a lesbian. They began an affair. "She was very motherly to me, very warm, and I was open to having a female lover. Her arms were a shelter, a refuge from all the bitterness of my life."

The older woman, Marge, wanted a commitment, but

Theresa was not ready for that. The affair ended when Marge left California.

Months later Theresa began an affair with a woman her age, whom she'd met at a political meeting. "I found that it was easy to relate to Pam. She had a great sense of humor and was very feminine. We had agreed to see other people, but she was very jealous, and the arrangement wasn't that easy."

The affair ended when Theresa "fell madly in love" with a male lawyer she met while working as a secretary at a radio station. She moved herself and her children to the East Coast to be with him.

She gave him everything she had, all the love and tenderness she'd always reserved for her children. She loved him because he was brilliant, dynamic, aggressive, and successful. He made her feel secure and cherished. Here was a powerful man who found her beautiful and exciting, unlike her husband. Although she was "only" an ex-housewife and secretary, he recognized her intelligence and charm. He was the first man in her life who listened to her and seemed crazy about her.

Five months after she and her children had moved in, he left. He realized, he said, that he was still involved with his wife, that he couldn't live with two young children underfoot, and that he wanted to be free to pursue other women.

Theresa could not afford to keep the apartment, and the man did not offer to help. She pulled herself together as best she could and moved to a cheaper building. She enrolled in night school to finish her bachelor's degree. "The whole summer I grieved," she said. "I consider this the biggest loss, the biggest disappointment of my life." She used to ride the subways and stare at the faces of the people around her, wondering if it was possible that any one of them was mourning as deeply as she was.

She continued to work, take care of her kids, and pursue her studies. She went out with a variety of men, but none of the relationships seemed fulfilling. She felt overwhelmed by her life—the care of two kids, the poverty, the struggle to put herself through school and hold a full-time job. She had always assumed that a man would love her and take care of her. What had happened to her dream? What was wrong with men? What was wrong with her?

"I was raised to believe that a man would sweep me off my feet," she said. "I adored my father as a young girl. He was a very romantic figure—an actor. Women adored him. He brought me up to feel that I was a princess.

"At this point in my life, I'm trying to understand my relationships with women. I do become excited by men. But I'm a needy person and need a lot of intimacy. I don't know if a man can give me that. Even if I married I think I would want a female lover in my life.

"In many ways a woman satisfies me more. In my head, the idea of making love to another woman is so exciting. I respond to the emotional aura as well as to the physical body. There's a very different sense of closeness. There's the knowledge that you've shared a similar experience. It's like looking into a mirror and finding yourself.

"I feel there are more women looking for commitment and a stable intimacy than men. And there are more women who will support my career desires, feel comfortable with my children, and share the household responsibilities."

Longing for comfort and a modicum of security, Theresa is pessimistic that she will ever meet a man with whom she can share the kind of interests, conversation, and understanding she has found in her relationships with women. "If I'd known then what I know now," she says, "I would not have left Marge. That kind of warmth is too hard to find. I wouldn't have walked away."

Lesbian Lovemaking

"What do female lovers do?" is a question asked by those who have not had homosexual experiences, those whose fantasies cannot take them through the locked doors of homoerotic love. What exactly happens?

Francine, a thirty-six-year-old clothing designer, told me this story.

She had been married to a stockbroker for eleven years. Her husband was too busy for anything more than minimal lovemaking, and as she crossed into her thirties, she felt more and more sexually frustrated. The feeling that she was missing something haunted her constantly. She dreamed of wild sexual orgies, of men passionately sweeping her off her feet and unleashing her dormant passions.

While she was dreaming, her husband became enamored of his secretary, and Francine found herself suddenly single. She met a woman in a class she was taking on the opera. "She was very feminine and confident," Francine said. "I was drawn to her."

One evening they had dinner in a New York restaurant. Downstairs there was a bar and a disco room, decorated in black and white. For the first time in her life Francine saw women holding hands, dancing close together in each other's arms. She experienced a mixture of feelings: confusion, repulsion, excitement, curiosity. . . .

Upstairs, there was a small, very pretty candle-lit restaurant, run by women for women only. Francine and her friend ordered duckling and wine and told each other about their lives. Gwen confessed she was bisexual.

Francine was too shy to ask her friend for any details. She wasn't sure what was expected of her. Yet, as she saw more and more of Gwen, she was drawn to her. She had fantasies of kissing her sensuous mouth, touching her long black hair.

Months passed.

One weekend at the beach together, they made love for the first time. There was a full moon outside, and they could hear the sounds of the waves crashing outside their window.

"We were in a double bed. It was the most natural thing in the world to hug and kiss," Francine said. She felt a little awkward but followed her friend's lead. She found herself tremendously excited by Gwen's smell, her skin, her touch.

They became lovers. "It was a very odd relationship," she explained. They would talk on the phone or see each other every day. However, in bed, Francine still could not reach orgasm. When Gwen relocated to Canada, the affair ended.

Francine decided, for a time, to be celibate. Months later, at a party, she met an architect in her early forties. They began to see each other. "She told me she wanted to make love to me. She said she would make me feel like no other had. I was intrigued. I still felt that I hadn't been released sexually."

The first time she went to bed with Roberta, she cried. "She was so tender, so appreciative. After we made love, she brought me chocolates. The next day she sent me a rose with a sweet note. She is an extremely loving woman."

As they became closer, Francine confessed that she'd never had an orgasm. "If I'd told a man that," she said, "he would have taken it as an insult to his manhood. He would not have understood but would have made me feel that it was my fault, that there was something wrong with me." Instead, Roberta told her not to worry, that she should just relax and eventually orgasm would occur.

"We began to make love every day," said Francine. "She would lie between my legs and move her tongue very gently in a circle around my clitoris. In the beginning I couldn't relax enough to *feel* her tongue. And when I couldn't come after ten or fifteen minutes, I would become extremely nervous and start to cry. I felt so frustrated!"

When she cried, Roberta would hold her in her arms and comfort her. "She had so much faith in my potential, and she was so understanding that for the first time in my life I began to relax and really trust the fact that she *liked* licking me; that she wouldn't ever become tired or bored, even if it took an hour or two hours for me to come.

"One night the miracle happened. I stopped worrying about *her* feelings and just began to concentrate on my own pleasure. I began to scream and I begged her not to stop, even if it took three hours, five hours! And then suddenly I had the experience . . . a convulsion in my stomach and a feeling of tremendous release." She paused. "That was one of the happiest days of my life."

"I gained a tremendous amount of self-esteem from our affair. I used to believe that female genitalia were ugly and smelly. However, Roberta really loved women—their bodies and smells. She told me my folds were like rose petals. If I ever make love to a man again, I know I will be a changed woman. I won't feel anxious about pleasing him. I know that I'm okay."

Francine was not the only woman to report that she had her first orgasm in the arms of a woman. Others echoed her experience.

> *I always thought I was frigid. Yet I really responded to Helen's touch. I was released by her passion, which was very different from my ex-husband's indifference.*
>
> *Helen will spend time with me. I have learned to come.*
>
> A thirty-nine-year-old cocktail waitress in St. Louis, Missouri

It's really fun playing with another woman's body.
My lover and I make love for at least an hour every
night. On the weekends we can hardly get out of
bed. I don't feel sexually frustrated with her, as I
felt with so many men. She doesn't rush me.

A thirty-two-year-old woman
who runs a plant shop

Researchers have come up with some surprising data on the sexuality of lesbian women. A study reported in *Psychology Today* stated that 98 percent of women involved in homosexual relationships experienced orgasm, as opposed to some 50 percent of heterosexual women. In their newest book, *Homosexuality in Perspective,* Dr. William Masters and Virginia Johnson support findings that homosexual women are often better lovers than heterosexual men. Homosexual women, they found, feel more open, uninhibited, and assertive with their partners than do heterosexual women. In heterosexual sex men make the decisions about when to begin and what position to use. They control the rhythm and duration of coitus, which often inhibits female orgasmic potential.

In lesbian lovemaking there is no final goal of male ejaculation. Without intercourse as the fixed main course, there is more of an emphasis on appetizers and desserts. The nuances are played out. Through oral sex, women focus on the clitoris, which is the seat of female sexual spasm.

My first homosexual affair was with a very free
lady. We used vibrators on each other's clitorises
to bring us to orgasm sometimes. That's fun.

A thirty-five-year-old sculptor

*When I had sex with my husband, it was over in
ten minutes. He wanted me to perform fellatio
for him, but he would never reciprocate. He was
convinced that women were dirty down there,
although he never had any shame about his own
body. I never had an orgasm during the nine years
we were married. I faked it.*

*I spend hours with my female lover. We never
use dildoes or any devices. We are just tender and
loving. We talk in bed, we cry, we laugh. There is
no shame.*

A thirty-nine-year-old
saleswoman

*I meet my neighbor during the day, when our
husbands are at work. For the first time I understand the pleasure of sex. Sex isn't dirty! I'm much
happier.*

A Catholic Long Island
homemaker

The female need for clitoral stimulation and prolonged lovemaking explains some of the data emerging
from this study. Female lovers seem to spend more time in
bed—kissing, fondling, stroking, massaging, teasing. Sex is
not simply genital intercourse but a more totally sensual
experience. The women can meet on a variety of levels: as
sisters, friends, mother-daughter, male-female. There are a
variety of roles to assume, needs to be confessed. In the
most uninhibited relationships, many combinations can be
played out.

Dr. Mildred Hope Witkin agrees that men and women
often have different sexual expectations. "Once a man has

had an orgasm," she says, "he doesn't want any more stimulation. He has a refractory period. The woman is very different. She can go on and on and on."

A Love Story

The house stood in the woods, solitary and majestic. Smoke poured from the chimney. Down the hill there was a small lake, dotted with park benches for lovers. Cars were parked here and there in the driveway up and down the desolate road.

It was a wonderful night for a party.

The party was being given by Sheila, a thirty-three-year-old woman in the advertising business. She had built and designed this house herself and invited her friends to celebrate its completion. Her new lover, Pat, a magazine illustrator, had done all the cooking. The fire blazed and music played. Women wore long flowing gowns or chic pants suits. People drank, talked, smoked, ate, necked, and danced. The only thing that made the party different was that the men were with men and the women with women.

However, the more I watched, the less "different" the party seemed. Another woman, an architect, sat with me. "See those two women," she said, pointing to a couple who looked exquisitely happy with each other. "They just found each other and they're madly in love. I'm so glad for them. Mary was so desperate and lonely before she met Jane." She paused. "There are great love stories that have taken place among women. Why don't you write about them?"

I bore witness to one love story. Both women are in their middle thirties, with relatively high-paying management positions in marketing. Although they keep their relationship secret for fear of losing their jobs, I was struck by their glowing happiness and their obvious contentment with each other and their life.

How did they meet?

On a double date. Martha was with her second husband. Bertha was with one of the husband's close friends. Martha, who had had two love affairs with women, said she felt an immediate attraction to Bertha. When they learned that they worked in the same area in downtown Los Angeles, they began driving back and forth to work together each day.

"I began to feel more and more strongly about Bertha," Martha said. "My husband was away on business for most of our marriage. We had only been together about a year. It was clear we were not going to stay together much longer, although we would remain friends."

One evening the two women went for a drink after work. "We were sitting in the cocktail lounge," Martha told me, "and I leaned over and said very fast, 'Bertha, I'm a lesbian and I'm falling in love with you.'" She was so nervous and had mumbled her words so fast that she wasn't even sure Bertha had understood.

Bertha did, although it took her a while to absorb this information. However, the more she thought about it, the more interested she became. All of her life she had felt like a misfit, unhappy with the rituals of dating. "I never understood why, if I wanted to see a boy, I had to wait for him to call me, rather than calling him myself." She said she felt men often expected her to be something that she wasn't.

She and Martha began an affair and fell deeply in love. "The first year we hardly got out of bed," Martha joked, "which is natural for any new couple. However, by the second year we were in a more normal phase. We realized that the relationship was going to last, and we could calm down."

They moved to the East Coast and established a home with Martha's nine-year-old son from her first marriage.

"People make such a fuss over homosexuality and children," Martha said. "We were so worried about my son. One night before dinner we sat him down and told him, 'Listen Larry, it's important that you understand that Bertha and I are in love with each other.' 'I know ma,' he said. 'What's for dinner?' We were so worried about our announcement, and he could not have cared less! And he's a perfectly normal boy who likes girls and receives a lot of love from two women who care about him, as well as from his father who sees him whenever he can."

One of their goals as a couple is to save up enough money so that they can retire in ten years and pursue their varied interests: music, theater, dance, literature, the study of nature.

"We have three bedrooms," Martha said. "One is for my son, and, theoretically, one is mine and one is Bertha's. Of course, we really share one bedroom, but the extra bedroom is for appearances. I won't hide the fact that I love Bertha, but I don't flaunt it either, especially with business colleagues."

How do their families feel about their relationship?

"Neither family ever asks a direct question, although if they did, we would tell the truth," Bertha said. "However, if they're more comfortable not discussing the issue, we respect their choice."

Both women wear identical butterfly rings, filled with tiny garnets and diamonds, as a symbol of their love. "We have seen society come a tremendously long way toward accepting homosexuality," Bertha said.

The Future

Despite Bertha's positive outlook and the tremendous strides we've made in the last fifteen years, the life of a gay woman is not easy. The necessity for secrecy is painful and frustrating. According to the Bell and Weinberg study, only 50 percent of both black and white women reported that their mothers and siblings knew about their sexual preference. And a dramatically smaller proportion of women said that they had told their fathers, neighbors, or employers about their choice. Hiding such a major and integral aspect of one's life exacts a huge emotional toll from many of these women.

Moreover, most lesbian women are still viewed primarily in sexual terms. Although they are mothers, homeowners, bank tellers, teachers, politicians, secretaries, churchgoers, and corporate women—paying their taxes and holding down jobs like the rest of us—they are still subject to the most incredible harassment and ridicule. Often their lives are lonely and isolated. It's difficult for a lesbian couple to mingle socially with heterosexual couples, and many find their social lives severely restricted.

Furthermore, homosexual women face severe economic problems, more so, in many cases, than their heterosexual sisters, since they can't rely on a man to bolster their lower salaries. "Now that we're living in a recession and the cost of living is going up, many money pressures are interfering with lesbian relationships," says Dr. Sang.

It is my hope, as we move in the 1980s, that lesbian women will gain the broad social acceptance they are entitled to. After listening to so many stories from women who have found happiness with other women, it seems patently unfair to deny them their right to love how and whom they choose.

CHAPTER
7

Out of the Kitchen, into the Office: The Over-Thirty Woman and Careers

On August 26, 1970, a historic event took place on Manhattan's Fifth Avenue. More than fifty thousand women gathered to voice their demands for equal opportunities and equal pay for equal work. And in the years that followed, huge numbers of women abandoned the kitchen and nursery to take jobs in factories, on assembly lines, in offices and corporations. What we have witnessed over this past decade is a social revolution, inexplicable to many traditionalists and proponents of the "typical" American nuclear family but much less surprising to the masses of women who jumped at the chance to work for pay. Today, women make up 42.1 percent of the country's total work force.

The over-thirty woman is experiencing the effects of this revolution in a more direct way than perhaps any other group. She grew up in an era when the successful woman was a wife, mother, and homemaker, and she came of age at a time when the successful woman was a corporate vice-president. It is, therefore, particularly appropriate to examine how women of this generation are faring in the work world only a little more than a decade after the 1970 march. How many over-thirty women are lunching on expense accounts, inhabiting corner offices, moving into the executive boardrooms? How many are still sitting in the typing pool?

The results of the survey were broad-ranging. Most women reported that they had just begun to think in terms of careers in their thirties. Many had started out as secretaries and assistants in their twenties, expecting to be married and taken care of by the time they were thirty. These women had been raised to depend on men for success and had only recently begun to think about success for themselves. Consequently, they were enrolling in schools to prepare for careers or reentering the work force at entry-level positions.

Other women, who were trained to be teachers and social workers, reported that they were anxious to change careers but didn't know how to go about it. A surprisingly large number of women wrote that they were thinking about starting their own businesses. Others were working as assistants, struggling to break into management. And at the top were a tiny group of excellers—successful, well-paid women who had reached new peaks of confidence and professionalism in their thirties.

As I studied the questionnaires and talked to hundreds of other women, several dominant themes emerged. First, most women feel that they're not achieving as much or as quickly as they feel they should. Second, sex and age discrimination continue to be a major block for women attempting the management transition. And third, many women reported that they lacked the confidence to move up the career ladder. The "good girl" rules have been too well instilled.

Success Stress

A large percentage of women reported suffering from low self-esteem as a result of the new pressure to succeed. "You *can* have it all," the media continue to tell us, but this exhortation neglects the real truth of our lives, which is the price women are paying—in anxiety and depression—as they try to meet new cultural expectations. The superwoman mystique is hard to escape.

> *I hate every birthday because it reminds me that I should have done more with my life than I have. Every time I read a women's magazine about a superwoman making fifty thousand dollars a year, I want to scream.*
>
> A thirty-nine-year-old production assistant earning fourteen thousand dollars a year

> *My husband expects me to go back to work and get a great job, earning a lot of money. But I haven't worked in twelve years, and when I went to an employment agency, all they asked me was "How fast can you type?"*
>
> A thirty-four-year-old homemaker

"Almost everybody has concrete things they expect to accomplish by the age of thirty," says Dr. Andrew DuBrin, a professor of behavioral science at the Rochester Institute of Technology. "For men and career-oriented women, being in the thirties is traumatic because it means you are no longer a nice kid with potential. Once you're thirty, you can no longer rationalize a lack of success as easily as before."

Although the concept of the thirties as a deadline decade may be realistic for some men, we cannot apply the same measurements when we judge the success of women. Our male peers spent their twenties climbing the career ladder; most of our generation took temporary jobs until we married or until our husbands finished school, then we settled down to raise our families. A career simply was not part of our life plans. We were, after all, patterning ourselves after our major role model—our mothers.

At an early, impressionable age we absorbed the message that women worked hard—but not for pay. Our mothers chauffeured us to ballet lessons, to school dances, to pizza parlors. They worked for the PTA, for the local hospital, for the March of Dimes. Their lives seemed busy and meaningful, and we aspired to that same kind of life—to be as giving, as loving, as supportive as our mothers were.

Many over-thirty women reported that they were actively discouraged from going to college because higher education was not considered necessary for girls. Of those women who did attend universities, most were encouraged to pursue liberal arts degrees or were channeled into traditional female fields like teaching and social service. During the 1960s women made up only 4 percent of law students, 1 percent of dentistry students, 1 percent of engineering students, and 6 percent of medical students. Even fewer women pursued business careers, and those who did rarely moved beyond the secretarial level.

In 1965, after I graduated from college, I went looking for a job. Although I had been an excellent student, and the recipient of two scholarships, employment agencies asked me only one question, "How fast can you type?"

When I patiently explained that I was looking for a "job with a future," I was not taken seriously. Surely, I was told, I would soon leave for the diaper brigade. I did not plan to have children, I would respond. Having been raised in a home with five younger children underfoot, I had no illusions about motherhood. *Anything* would be easier. I wanted to work, and I needed to make money.

Invariably, the (male) interviewer would be shocked. Not have children! Oh my dear, I was sure to change my mind. All women wanted children!

For two years I did secretarial work, hoping for a break. My male college pals were already two years ahead. Finally, I landed a terrific job as a reporter for a small newspaper chain. The editor who hired me was a woman who had herself begun as a secretary twenty-five years before. She took a chance on me and became my first mentor. Although I started at six thousand dollars a year, half of what Allen, the male reporter across the hall made, I said nothing about the inequity. I was so thrilled at the opportunity I would have worked for nothing. Yet, three years later, I was one of the women marching down Fifth Avenue, demanding equal pay for equal work.

The catalyst for the 1970 march occurred in 1964, with passage of Title 7 of the Civil Rights Act, prohibiting discrimination on the basis of sex. Although Title 7 received formal backing from the Equal Opportunities Commission, which was formed in 1969, the courts did not rule on the 1964 law until 1971. And it was not until January of 1973 that American Telephone and Telegraph, the nation's largest employer of women, signed a consent decree, paving the way for true equality for women.

The company was found to have put women hired between 1965 and 1972 into dead-end jobs, although they had slotted men for fast-track management development programs. As a result of the landmark decree, the company had to single out women with potential and offer them career opportunities in management equal to those their male counterparts were receiving. They also had to pay women seventy-three million dollars in back salaries.

Only since 1970 has there been a concerted effort to open up employment opportunities for women on a broad scale. A wonderful book called *The Decade of Women,* by the staff of *Ms.* magazine and published by Putnam, points out the following amazing breakthroughs women have made in only one decade.

1970: The first Lutheran woman pastor is ordained.

The first all women's professional tennis tour is scheduled.

The first women generals are commissioned—Elizabeth Holsington, Director of the Women's Army Corps, and Anna Mae Hays, chief of the Army Nurse Corps.

Forty-six editorial staff women win a settlement of their suit charging sex discrimination at *Newsweek* magazine.

1971: The U.S. Supreme Court rules that companies cannot refuse to hire mothers with small children unless the same policy applies to fathers.

The New York Board of Education votes to allow high school girls and boys to compete in noncontact sports.

Girls are appointed Senate pages for the first time in U.S. history.

1972: The University of Minnesota lets women into its marching band.

Sally Priesand is the first woman ordained as a rabbi.

1973: Women are admitted to the U.S. Coast Guard officer-candidate program.

1974: The Merchant Marine Academy and the National Little League Baseball Inc. agree to admit females.

1975: The Pentagon outlaws automatic discharge of pregnant women from the armed services.

Joellen Drag is the Navy's first female helicopter pilot. She later files a successful class action suit against the Navy for refusing to permit women pilots to land at sea.

1976: The National Aeronautics and Space Administration (NASA) announces it will accept women for astronaut training. It had rejected qualified women in the past.

The Supreme Court rules that pregnant women cannot automatically be denied unemployment benefits in the weeks before and after childbirth.

Sarah Caldwell becomes the first woman to conduct at the Metropolitan Opera after Beverly Sills refuses to sing unless Caldwell conducts.

1977: NBC signs a $1.7 million agreement with EEOC for back pay and affirmative action programs for women.

Reader's Digest agrees to pay more than $1.5 million back salaries, and offers immediate salary increases to 2,600 female employees.

1978: Kansas City, Missouri, is the site of the first Women's Jazz Festival.

Golfer Nancy Lopez wins $161,235, setting a record for a rookie, male or female.

Monsanto Textiles Company pays Barbara Taibi $10,000 in the largest individual settlement to date in a sexual harassment suit.

More women than men enter college for the first time in American history.

1979: More than 290 women hold seats on the boards of major corporations, an increase of almost 100% since 1975 according to Catalyst, a career service organization.

Furthermore, educational opportunities for women increased dramatically during the early 1970s. By 1974 women made up 23 percent of law students, 11 percent of dentistry students, 6 percent of engineering students, and 22 percent of medical students. Quite a contrast to the figures for 1960! (See page 165.) This surge in enrollment can be traced to the fact that Women's Equity Action League (WEAL) officer Dr. Bernice Sandler filed the first formal charge of sex discrimination against the University of Maryland under Executive Order 11246 in January 1970. In the next two years suits against three hundred other colleges were instituted.

As a result of these impressive achievements and the unprecedented push for equal opportunities, women can seriously consider their own potential and define career dreams in a way never before possible. But it is important to bear in mind that we're only ten years down the road. We have only just *begun* to break down discriminatory barriers. Therefore, we cannot measure ourselves according to deadlines that have nothing to do with our personal histories. Had we been encouraged to plan a career from the time we were little girls, had we been taught that it was within our rights to be competitive and aggressive, it is very likely that we would see many more successful career women in their thirties.

Moreover, as the pioneers of a social revolution, we are the first generation to question the rigid social structures that have supported American life. Traditionally, the decisions our parents and grandparents made in their twenties set the pattern for the rest of their lives. Today, both men and women have much greater freedom to change the course of their lives midstream. An early decision to be a doctor, a lawyer, a homemaker, a teacher, does not necessarily lock you into that role for the rest of your life. An individual may have two, three, even four careers in a lifetime.

Over-thirty women who are just beginning to develop new career identities must not allow themselves to feel like failures because they haven't yet achieved their goals. They must realize they are in crowded company. Measuring ourselves according to the traditional male timetable is both harmful and counterproductive. Once we set our own standards, we can broaden our perspective and spend our thirties planning for the second half of our lives.

Women Need a Different Timetable for Success

Daniel J. Levinson, the psychologist who studied adult male development, discovered that successful men went through a novice stage between the ages of seventeen and thirty-three. The task of this period was to define their dream of adult accomplishment and find a mentor.

Half of the biologists he interviewed for his book *The Seasons of a Man's Life* reported that their career aspirations began with the realization of a powerful, exciting dream; in most cases, a dream that began as early as high school. The fifteen-year novice period was the transition between that dream and its fulfillment.

Using Levinson's data as a guide, a woman who defines a career goal in her thirties can expect that, on the average, it will take her fifteen years to achieve that goal. To expect progress sooner is not realistic. In fact, it may even take her five to ten years longer if she has children to raise or if she faces serious sex discrimination. A thirty-five-year-old woman who decides she wants to pursue a career as a stockbroker, for example, will probably achieve the peak of her success in her late forties or early fifties.

Accepting this new timetable is important for any woman in transition. "I'll be dead by the time I reach success," one woman joked, when I told her about my new timetable. But that's not true. Statistics tell us that the average woman lives until she is seventy-seven, and many live longer. Even if we achieve success in our fifties, we still have twenty good years to enjoy its blessings. And in the meantime the learning process is fascinating and fun.

Certainly, there are women who have achieved phenomenal success at a young age. But these women had formulated their career dream in their late teens or early twenties and spent the requisite fifteen years developing their careers. Once women see their personal struggle within the larger historical context, they can approach their individual situations with greater courage and hope.

Discrimination

The 1980s promise to be a difficult decade, particularly for the over-thirty woman, because there will be fewer good jobs available and competition from a younger generation of women who were not at the battlefront but who are reaping the rewards of our fight. According to *Business Week* magazine, "Recent college graduates and young managers make salaries equal to those of men in comparable jobs" but that "women who started their careers seven to ten years ago still lag far behind."

For the over-thirty reentering woman, age discrimination may be an even more serious problem than sex discrimination.

I wanted to work as an executive secretary to a
television producer, but he hired a twenty-two-
year-old blonde instead. I know I am more com-
petent, but he was turned off by the fact that I had
two children. I was discriminated against, but I
can't prove it.

A thirty-nine-year-old divorcée

I was very hopeful about getting into the work
force after years of being at home, but I became
very discouraged. One man implied I was over the
hill and that I'd be lucky to get any job.

A thirty-seven-year-old former
actress

"For all the talk about change," says Louise Howe,
author of *Pink Collar Workers*, "the vast majority of
women are still doing what they did at the turn of the century. There's less opportunity for noncollege women to
move up, because college women are getting the kinds of
jobs noncollege women used to get. Today, you need a
master's for the kind of job you used to need a college
degree for."

Figures show that 80 percent of the females who work
are clustered in low-paid, dead-end jobs. They are clerks,
bank tellers, secretaries, waitresses, factory workers, and
department store saleswomen. Only one in twenty women
is in an executive or management position. At present,
women hold fewer than 2 percent of the directorships of
top American corporations, and fewer than 1 percent of
top management posts.

One might argue that the reason there are so few
women in managerial positions is that women have not yet
learned to be effective managers. However, women are

naturals for management—*more so than men*—according to the prestigious Johnson O'Connor Research Foundation, Inc. This nonprofit organization, with twelve testing facilities scattered across the country, has tested thousands of people of all ages since 1922.

The institute listed twenty-two basic aptitudes necessary for a good manager. In fourteen of these there were absolutely no differences between the sexes. Of the eight aptitudes that showed sexual differences, women excelled in six, men only in two.

Aptitudes in which there were no discernible sex differences include:
- analytical reasoning
- foresight
- inductive reasoning
- memory for design
- number memory
- objective and subjective personality
- general knowledge as measured by vocabulary tests

The most important aptitude men excel in is structural visualization. This aptitude is central to the technical and scientific professions such as engineering, architecture, surgery, mechanics, and building. The average young man completes the test work sample in 1.75 minutes, the young female in 2.75 minutes. (Erector sets and building blocks—toys traditionally given to boys—help build this aptitude in young children.)

Women excel in:
- graphoria or accounting aptitude, which is an asset in auditing, statistical, and actuarial work.
- ideaphoria, which measures the rate of flow of new ideas and the ability to persuade. This aptitude is helpful in professions such as sales, teaching, writing, or advertising.

• observation, which reflects a person's ability to perceive changes. It is helpful in insurance adjustment, police work, and plant inspection. On the test sample, the average woman amasses 88 points, the man 85.

• abstract visualization, which refers to ability to deal with abstract problems, ideas, and principles. This aptitude is an asset in banking, industrial management, politics, and writing. Whereas 75 percent of all women possess abstract visualization, only 50 percent of men do.

Theoretically, the institute acknowledges, there ought to be more women than men in management. The fact that there aren't indicates that discriminatory attitudes toward women still exist.

A qualified television executive wrote in to say, "I told the men at my office I wanted to be a station manager. They responded that there were no women station managers and that it would be a long time before there would be one."

A retail chain store executive making fifty thousand dollars a year was shooting to become a general merchandise manager, a position that pays about one hundred thousand dollars a year. "When I went in to the president to talk about my career plans," she reported, "I was told that it would be impossible to achieve that goal because I am a woman. I became so angry I quit on the spot and within a month moved to another company. In the retail business, all the people at the top are still men."

A female filmmaker said she believed that if she were a man, she would be able to get the money needed for her projects. "The biggest problem for the woman artist is money. Many of the men who have the money to invest don't trust their wives, and they certainly don't trust other women. Practically all of the directors and producers in Hollywood are still men."

Certainly, women have made token breakthroughs in

the business world. Yet when women shoot for top positions, they often find themselves closed out. And those women who have had the courage to sue discover that the courts are backlogged with discriminatory suits that will take two to three years, if not longer, to resolve. This in itself is very discouraging.

Until women win the Equal Rights Amendment and organize on a massive scale, we will continue to see a stepped-up backlash against affirmative action. "I think it's worse in the corporations now than it was five years ago," one executive told me. "Because we haven't won the Equal Rights Amendment, men see us as weak—as people who can be pushed around. They are sick of hearing about women's rights. They want the issue to go away. It is still the rare man who can stand having a woman compete against him and win."

Unfortunately, men are not the only ones who perceive women as pushovers, especially within the context of the business world. Far too many women hold that view themselves, and consequently they don't have the confidence to fight the necessary battles, to push as hard as they have to, or to band together to help themselves in business.

Breaking Out of the "Good Girl" Mode

The fact is that many women simply don't know how to be winners. The traditional values that are part and parcel of our "good girl" training—modesty, passivity, humility, naïveté—work against us in the business world. By dedicating ourselves to pleasing others and subordinating our own egos, we've become victims, and in the classic stance of any powerless, enslaved group, we fight back in the only way we know—by oblique complaints, through attempts to arouse sympathy for our plight as poor, helpless victims. We mistake the annoyed pity that the strong accord the weak for love and genuine sympathy. "Look," we say, "look how we're abused, doing all the work for our boss while he gets all the credit." We glory in our martyrdom, and the payoff is in the reinforcement of our traditional role of self-effacement and helplessness.

How often have you seen a woman take on extra work without seeking any more tangible compensation than a pat on the back? And when that pat doesn't come, and it often doesn't, she has another opportunity to feel put upon and abused.

How often have you heard women talking about their bosses in a slightly amused, superior tone? They laugh at their boss's silly foibles, his petty nature. They try to hang onto some measure of self-esteem by holding themselves above it all—but at what price?

The winning style, on the other hand, is linked to feelings of mastery and evidences itself in a kind of arrogant boasting. Businessmen routinely brag about their successes but rarely, if ever, mention their failures. Most women, however, are impelled to discuss their failures, dissecting and examining them at length, seeking sympathy and understanding from others.

If women want to achieve true equality in the workplace, they have to fight their addiction to the victim role. And they can begin by seeking out and modeling themselves after those women who have broken out of the "good girl" mode.

The Success Syndrome: Successful Women as Role Models

When I began this study, I particularly wanted to zero in on the characteristics of high-achieving women. I wanted to find out what they had in common, why they were so successful, what they could teach other women. I chose to interview five women: Sally Frame, the thirty-four-year-old vice-president and general merchandise manager for Ann Taylor Stores; Lynn Salvage, the thirty-four-year-old former president of the First Women's Bank, now president and chief administrator of Katherine Gibbs; Suzanne Bauman, a thirty-five-year-old filmmaker, whose film *Spirit Catcher* won a red ribbon at the American Film Festival, and who has just produced *The Artist Was a Woman* for public television; Margery Waxman, the thirty-six-year-old former director of the Federal Trade Commission, now general counsel for the Office of Personnel Management; and Kay Wight, the thirty-seven-year-old vice-president of compliance and administration for CBS Television Sports. And despite the obvious differences in their professions and backgrounds, a number of common traits emerged.

First, the excelling woman learned to be a competitive winner rather than a polite lady. Raised according to a male model of success, she was encouraged to be aggressive rather than passive, to seek out competition and achievement. *The high achiever has an intense desire to be first, to win, to be outstanding.*

> *As a child, I was encouraged to be a figure skater. When I figure skated, I didn't play. I wanted to be the best.*

Lynn Salvage

> *I was brought up to excel. My mother raised me to believe I could do anything I wanted to do. I was a Phi Beta Kappa at Vassar and received a scholarship to the Institute of Film and TV at New York University.*

Suzanne Bauman

These women were raised to feel comfortable with the idea of achievement. In contrast, the vast majority of our generation were raised to be supporters and nurturers, to put the bulk of their energies into their children, husbands, bosses' careers, or community involvements. For example, a thirty-four-year-old secretary from Cailfornia wrote in to complain that it had taken her "fourteen years just to become a secretary." Analyzing her family background, she said that her parents saw her as a dreamer who should "quit thinking bigger than her brains" and "marry the first man who proposed." They did not encourage her to dream big dreams or to push herself forward.

Second, *excelling women had early successful role models with whom they were able to identify.*

> *I was raised with a priority on academic performance. My grandfather, a professor of economics and math, was a great influence on me.*
>
> Lynn Salvage

> *I grew up wanting to be Eleanor Roosevelt.*
>
> Margery Waxman

Third, *all these women made work—rather than love—their first priority.* All have incredible energy and discipline, love to work, and put in inordinately long hours at their jobs, just like the high-achieving male. When necessary, they sacrifice their personal lives for their careers. With the exception of Suzanne Bauman who has been raising four children since 1975, none of the other women have children. Because motherhood is such arduous work, it is the rare mother who can achieve career success in her thirties. Indeed, motherhood is a career in its own right.

*I work a twelve-hour day, six days a week. I don't
like long vacations. After one week I'm itching to
get back to work.*

Sally Frame

*I put all my energy into my career. I have always
worked six or seven days a week, twelve to fourteen
hours a day. I would get into my office at seven-
thirty in the morning and work till eight at night.
I rarely took vacations. On one three-week vacation, I went to Harvard for a course in management.*

Margery Waxman

Fourth, *all five focused in on their careers in the beginning of their twenties.* Like Levinson's successful men,
they spent fifteen years working toward fulfillment of that
early dream.

*I recognized my ambition when I was a junior in
college and majored in radio and television
journalism. A woman who had a television career
spoke on our campus, and I admired her so much
I took her as a role model. I wanted to go to New
York and be just like her.*

Kay Wight

*If anyone had told me I would be in fashion when
I was a teenager, I would have said no. I hated to
go shopping—but when I was in college, I had a
part-time job at Lord & Taylor's and loved the
way the store smelled. I also liked the exciting pace,
especially around the holidays.*

> *When I graduated, I was offered a job as*
> *assistant department manager, and a female took*
> *me under her wing. When she left, I got her job. I*
> *was the youngest department manager Lord &*
> *Taylor ever had.*

Sally Frame

Fifth, *the exceller has spent more than ten years de-*
veloping her career and learning her business.

> *Many men took me under their wings. I listened a*
> *lot. I learned the tools of my business, how to figure*
> *rate of sale and buy the trend.*

Sally Frame

> *I started out as a secretary. I tried to change secre-*
> *tarial jobs every six months, to get a good overview*
> *of the company. You can move all over this way*
> *without hurting yourself professionally.*

Kay Wight

Sixth, *the exceller learned to take risks at an early age,*
either by competing for the honor society or cheerleading
or the softball team. Throughout her life, risk taking is a
pattern.

> *My first risk was with a little terrycloth robe. I*
> *noticed we sold forty one Saturday. So I moved*
> *them to a prominent position on the floor and*
> *decided to make this robe my goldmine. I got on*
> *the phone Monday morning and guessed how many*
> *more we needed. We sold and sold that robe.*

Sally Frame

I put two thousand dollars of my own money into making my first film.

Suzanne Bauman

Seventh, *high achievers are team players rather than queen bees.*

One of my strengths is that I am able to get along with a great number of people with different interests and personalities. I am excellent at motivating people and understanding their needs.

Margery Waxman

I believe in helping other women, something I learned as a little girl in the Brownies and Girl Scouts.

Kay Wight

Finally, *the exceller works hard to develop contacts and maintain a high level of visibility in her field,* generally by becoming professionally involved in a variety of organizations. Kay Wight, for example, is the affirmative action chair for American Women in Radio and Television and sits on the executive committee and board of directors for the American Cancer Society in New York. She is also a member of Women in Communication, the National Organization for Women, and the National Academy of Television Arts and Sciences.

Although the vast majority of over-thirty women have not reached the level of success shared by these five women, their stories are important to the rest of us. As role models, they provide a context for our own development. Obviously, women can't turn back the clocks and change the kind of upbringing they had, but they can, in their thirties, work to develop many of the crucial characteristics needed for success. They can begin by taking their own development seriously, devoting themselves to achieving their goals, and taking full responsibility for their progress. Many women can be as successful as these excellers by the time they reach their fifties.

Women in Transition

The greatest number of my respondents were women in various stages of transition, and their feelings about the career issue ranged from excitement, hope, and exhilaration to depression and despair.

> I was admitted to law school when I was thirty-five and surprised to see that I could do the work. Life was hard because I had a child to support, my father was hospitalized, and my best friend had just died. I was lonely and tired, but I kept struggling to graduate, and am now finishing feeling optimistic and hopeful about the future.
>
> A thirty-eight-year-old
> Californian

> I took an assertiveness course at our local YWCA, and then I decided to get a real estate license. I just started to make excellent money, and I love the freedom of the field plus the people contact.
>
> A Lutheran divorcée

> On my thirtieth birthday, I had a feeling of absurdity because I was still in school. I felt trapped in a cage, but then I saw the door was open. I

*stopped work on my dissertation and decided I
really wanted to do silversmithing, having studied
jewelry design in Mexico. I feel excited and hopeful
about this new career.*

A thirty-two-year-old
Alaskan correspondent

*I started out as a secretary in an insurance office.
Then I went into civil service as a stenographer. My
experience in insurance qualified me for a claims
examiner position in the legal office, and then I
made a lateral move into the procurement field. I
have just been promoted to contracting officer.*

A thirty-six-year-old divorced
mother in Illinois, and a
member of Federally
Employed Women

These women are homemakers reentering the work
force for the first time in more than ten to fifteen years:
they are secretaries hoping to work up to a management
position; they are teachers and social workers wanting to
change careers; they are women opening their own businesses; they are women returning to medical, law, and business school. Although many are finding their initial forays
into the work world difficult, the majority are hopeful, committed, and willing to work hard.

The Reentering Woman

After a long hiatus in the home, the woman who re-
enters the job market may find the experience exciting or
demoralizing, depending on her approach and her own level
of confidence. Many women reported that they began with a

visit to an employment agency, and most agreed that it was a very negative experience. Even when they had more to offer than their ability to hit the typewriter keys, agencies were unwilling to consider them for anything other than secretarial or clerical positions.

Starting out as a secretary in an interesting field can be a good choice for the reentering woman. Other successful reentering women started by taking stock of their own situation and interests before they even began seriously looking for work. Many banded together with other reentering women, meeting on a regular basis to share their problems, pool their resources, and offer necessary moral support for one another. When initial job-hunting experiences are negative, the anxiety and depression women feel often manifests itself in inertia, and in isolation that inertia feeds on itself. In a group situation, women are less likely to retreat, to put off making important phone calls or following up on interesting ads.

As a career counselor, I found the group approach extremely helpful. I began my own groups by asking the women to list ten successes in their lives that were most important to them. Invariably, many respond by saying, "Ten! I'll be lucky if I can think of three." For many women it is the first time they have ever taken stock of themselves, and their initial anxiety turns quickly to excitement as a surprising number of successes come to mind.

It is an important and useful technique because it offers a means of probing one's strengths and weaknesses. For example, a woman may discover that she felt most successful when she was entertaining guests, doing volunteer work at an old-age home, gardening, or studying French. These discoveries are meaningful in that they offer her a direction.

The woman who enjoys entertaining might consider a career as a banquet, hotel, or restaurant manager or as a social director for a club or organization. The woman who enjoyed studying French might seek a position as a bilingual secretary or a French tutor. She might enjoy working in an art gallery that features impressionist painting, or opening up her home to French students. The woman who enjoys working with old people might train to become a nurse or a doctor. The successful gardener might open up a florist shop, run a landscape business, or begin a local lecture series on gardening.

A woman who enjoys people contact and wants to earn good money should consider a high-paying field like sales. When Carla was thirty-six, she took a job in an insurance company. She learned everything she could, and on her own she persuaded three young couples in her apartment complex to buy insurance from her. Then she went in to her boss and said, "See, I can sell. I want a position as an insurance salesperson." She got it, too.

Carla's experience illustrates the importance of taking risks rather than waiting for someone to notice your potential. She was shrewd and she took the initiative. She planned her strategy and came in with a package that was difficult for her boss to turn down.

When a woman is in doubt about goals, returning to school can be a wonderful choice because it expands awareness of one's untapped talents and capabilities. My friend Margalo struggled as a divorced mother to bring up two children alone, yet she still managed to acquire a bachelor's degree and go on to law school. Now in her thirties she is on her way to a bright, new future. Many women who go back to school in their thirties discover something very important—that they're much smarter than they think they are.

Before making any decision about returning to school, reentering the work force, or changing careers, a woman should research the job market as thoroughly as possible.

And she should not limit herself to the occupations traditionally reserved for women. Today, particularly, industries previously dominated by men are actively searching for qualified women. According to Molly Hawk Daniel, "The future looks brightest for women in nontraditional fields." In an article called "What Are the Jobs of the 80s?" in a recent issue of *Ms.* magazine, she writes: "Electronics, structural engineering, and the aerospace industry are among those that so far haven't been attracting enough women workers to satisfy affirmative actions needs . . . jobs in commercial banking, auto sales, and restaurant and hotel management are increasing. The insurance industry is currently hiring more women—as actuaries and underwriters—than any other industry . . . the computer field promises to be the biggest employer in the coming decade."

Many reentering women neglect their most valuable resource in a job search—people. But friends, relatives, and acquaintances, particularly those who are well established in the business world, can provide valuable information and contacts. "Good girls" are often reluctant to ask for help, fearing that they will be "using" people. Men have long understood the importance of contacts, of the "old boy" network, and many successful men started their climb to the top with the help of a college roommate, a neighbor, a golf partner. The woman who is interested in exploring her options must begin by talking to as many business people as she knows to learn about job titles, pay scales, and career paths. According to studies, 80 percent of the good jobs are acquired through personal contact. If a woman impresses someone with her energy, ambition, intelligence, and verbal or managerial skills, she may be offered a job.

Another useful technique for women is the five-year plan. Every woman should take the time to consider and answer the following questions as part of that plan: What risks should I be taking that might benefit me now? What new contacts should I be making? How much am I worth now (according to industry standards), and what can I do within a year to increase my worth? What kinds of projects should I be developing? How can I become more visible? What problems do I have with people, and how can I resolve them? Who are my competitors, and how can I outwit them? Once a woman begins to manage her career more assertively, she will be on her way to achieving her goals. Both the reentering woman and the career changer must remember to be optimistic, and to expect the transition to take two to five years.

Owning Your Own Business

For many women owning a business is a dream long cherished in secret. To turn an avocation into a vocation— whether it be knitting, antiques, food, books—seems an ideal way to escape the pressures and competition of the corporate rat race. Up until very recently, only 2 percent of all businesses have been owned and operated by women. But judging from the results of this study, it is a choice I suspect more and more women will be making in the coming decade. There is no doubt that it is a risky venture— 80 percent of all new businesses fail—but the number of success stories I heard about was encouraging.

If you can afford to take the risk, owning your own business can offer security, power, status, and money. "As long as we are a capitalistic nation," says Dr. Nancy Stevens, director of career counseling and placement at Hunter College in New York, "women should be interested in business."

How does the over-thirty woman begin? I first heard of thirty-eight-year-old Susan Axelrod, owner of a successful food service business called Love and Quiches, from my father, who manages country clubs on Long Island where

Susan has her business. We met at O'Neal's Baloon, one of the many Manhattan restaurants Love and Quiches services.

For Susan the impetus was basic—a need to use her energy and talent in a meaningful way. A friend suggested that they go into the food service business together. Until that time Susan had been a traditional homemaker, with two young children underfoot. During the years she spent at home she had found an outlet in cooking so the food service idea seemed perfect. "I was stuck in the house so I learned to cook, and I loved it," she told me. The two women decided to make quiches because they "are a great alternative on a menu to hamburger."

They formed a corporation and set up their dough-rolling equipment in Susan's garage. The first restaurant they approached was O'Neal's Baloon in Manhattan.

"They said no at first," Susan told me, "but I just kept talking, and eventually they said they would try our quiche."

Their sample was a success, and they received their first order.

For the first two years the business did not make any money. "We did everything wrong. We didn't control our costs or shop wholesale. We didn't put enough of our money into it. We were doing everything ourselves. I had quiches spread out all over the living room. We didn't have proper packaging for our delivery. We were losing accounts as fast as we were getting them."

Susan decided to buy out her partner, throw out the inventory, move into a storefront, and start over. "Luckily I had a lot of goodwill going for me, which was a miracle considering that we had given such miserable service."

She also had the business name, which everyone adored. The inspiration came from a sampler her partner's aunt had given them. Their registered trademark is a fat lady with a rolling pin. Susan's business cards are hot pink.

Little by little she learned the business. "I did tours of

restaurants to assess what they needed and find out how I could service them. I attended trade shows, read books, and talked to anyone I could. I learned figures. I can work out projections. I believe I can run *any* kind of business now."

She began to make profits, and as she did, she invested them—in employees ("Any time you can pay a person to save you time, the savings are threefold") and a commercial freezer ("You can freeze two hundred and forty pies at once").

She perfected her quiche batter, and she now makes twenty different kinds in five sizes. She also added a full line of pastries and desserts, among them a chocolate and carrot cake. "In the food business, you have to know what's new and offer it too."

Among her forty-five employees is a baker and a small sales force that does cold calls and sends out samples. Susan concentrates on product development, making decisions, and running the business. "I'm the computer brain. I tour the entire business every day, checking up on people and reading the invoices."

Susan works about twelve hours a day. She gets up at five-thirty and starts her morning with a phone call to her baker. Then she and her husband, who has joined the business, leave in separate cars. Her housekeeper makes dinner, and she and her husband get into bed at seven-thirty, where they watch TV, read, and talk over the day.

She has just bought a building and plans to expand her business. "In our industry, you have to grow bigger or your competition will outgrow you. I want to pass on the business, or perhaps even sell my business for several million dollars in ten years. I don't always want to work so hard. I say, don't do it for the glory. Do it for the money."

How has her marriage changed? "We always were best friends," she says. "My son and daughter both work in the business. We spend weekends on the boat we share with another couple. Last year my husband and I went on a marvelous two-week gourmet tour through the south of France, tax deductible. It was the best vacation of our lives."

For forty-one-year-old Betty Burge, who runs an antique and furniture reproduction business, business success came about "accidentally." The daughter of a socially prominent family, she attended Sarah Lawrence College and married an antiques dealer at twenty-four. She had two children, but she did not stay home to bring them up. She worked for her husband, selling to customers, and employed nurses and housekeepers. In her early thirties she became very dissatisfied. "That seems to be a time to examine the direction your life is taking. You feel like it's a last chance. At this time I stopped selling for my husband. I wanted to do something more fulfilling. He was very reluctant for me to leave our business. He wanted me there because he wanted me there. He was not receptive to my needs. He wasn't concerned that I wasn't happy doing what he was doing. He just thought I *should* be happy.

"It took a long period of discussion to get him to agree to my leaving. It was the first time I had ever really fought for my own needs, and it was very difficult. I went to art school and began designing custom-made jewelry for a small group of clients. I loved doing what I was doing."

Her life took a sudden, unexpected turn when her husband died three years later. She was a widow in her late thirties and faced overwhelming responsibilities.

She decided she had to take over her husband's business. "It was very frightening to be responsible for so much. I spent sleepless nights when I faced certain business problems. I went into therapy to cope with dealing with the loss and the problems my children were having."

Gradually, however, she began to perceive how capable she was. "I'm a totally different person since my husband died. I have not only proven to myself that I could make a business run but that I am doing *better* than my husband. I have an enormous sense of pride in myself." She paused. "If I hadn't been left alone, I would be very different from what I am today. My husband would have been my chief means of support. I wouldn't be so career-oriented.

"I'm much more aware now of how people try to manipulate me because I'm a woman. I never wanted to be a tough businesswoman. I didn't want to change my feminine personality for this job. But every now and then I catch someone trying to take advantage of my light touch. However, I will not be manipulated. Even though I have a soft voice, I am demanding and I can get angry."

Looking back at her life, she can chart her maturity, the strength and understanding that she has acquired. "I could never have handled my forties ten years ago. I thought being thirty was horrible. Thirty seemed so old when I was twenty-nine. And when I was thirty-five and thought of being forty, that was terrible too. However, by forty I had changed so much that it felt completely different than I had expected it to. I am so much more secure.

"Perhaps because I matured very late emotionally, I feel younger than I am. However, everything is a matter of life awareness. I have a friend who's twenty-three, and her mother is about the same age I am. Her mother came from a small town and was in the house all the time. I've been all over the world. I feel I have much more in common with the daughter than with the mother. I feel much more attractive now than I did ten years ago, and much more attractive than twenty years ago. When I think about myself in my twenties, I was simply an empty-headed superficial girl."

It's never too late to live out lost dreams; that should be the motto at every over-thirty woman. And stories like Susan's and Betty's prove it. They themselves took the responsibility for making their dreams come true. In their thirties they developed the same qualities characteristic of high-achieving women. They conquered their guilt for ambitious strivings, learned the ins and outs of their respective businesses, and took whatever risks were necessary. And they were rewarded by discovering vast reservoirs of untapped potential.

Once women start believing in themselves—in their potential, intelligence, energy, and creativity—they will be invincible.

8

The Joy of Money

During my first marriage, although my husband and I both worked, he handled all our money. He paid the bills and made various investments, and at the time I was perfectly content with the arrangement. Frequently, he tried to talk to me about the stock market, but I never really listened. As soon as he started to describe a stock, my mind would go blank. I felt that the subject had nothing to do with my life; after all, the stock market was for men. Moreover, raised as a Christian, I believed that money could not buy happiness, that it was, in fact, the root of all evil. I felt that I was somehow "above" involving myself with money. I had no idea that money could help me, could be my friend.

I had to learn about the importance of money the hard way. The year after my divorce, while I was struggling to establish myself as a free-lance writer, I earned about six thousand dollars. And for the first time in my life I had to worry about paying the rent and meeting my expenses, minimal as they were. My growing pride in coping with other aspects of living alone was undermined by my difficulty in meeting even the most basic financial obligations. I felt vulnerable, and I fantasized constantly that a man would come along to take care of me.

Three years later I earned fifty thousand dollars, and although I felt much more powerful and independent with money in my pocket, my years of relative poverty hadn't taught me much about handling it wisely. At one point during that year, when I was feeling in need of some pampering, I checked into a plush New York hotel for a three-day stay at one hundred and ten dollars a day. How much wiser I would have been to put that money into a savings account or invest it in one way or another.

Sadly, as the results of this study indicate, my experiences are an all-too-common theme among women in their thirties. When it comes to money, we are as helpless as newborn infants. A single friend of mine, who earns over thirty thousand dollars a year, has never learned how to budget her money or control her impulsive spending. Each month she faces a period of tremendous anxiety, worrying about how she can pay her rent and her bills. Consequently, she's desperate to meet a man who will rescue her.

Why are so many over-thirty women facing severe financial difficulties? The answer is twofold. First, growing up in the 1950s, we were schooled in a domestic mentality. We were not expected, or even encouraged, to learn how to plan budgets, invest wisely for our children's college educations, or buy our own homes. That was men's work. Even if our mothers worked, more often than not they turned their paychecks over to our fathers who, in return, doled out a weekly household allowance.

When Prince Charming came along to sweep us off our feet, he would provide us with a home, a car, with the money for food, clothing, vacations. There was no reason for us to worry our pretty little heads about such matters. Math, like science and shop, were subjects that boys traditionally excelled in. And if we were interested in these "serious" subjects, we learned not to talk about them, especially to boys. If we wanted to be popular, we couldn't encroach on male territory.

Unfortunately, we learned our lesson all too well: most women of our generation know very little about money—even those who have been working for years. It was not surprising to hear that a majority of women in this study had only begun to think seriously about money in their thirties, often because a divorce had precipitated a financial crisis.

Furthermore, despite the strides we've made in breaking into the business world in recent years, women's salaries remain consistently—and shockingly—lower than those of their male peers. The over-thirty woman who wants to make her own way in the world may be in for a rude shock when she discovers that a job will not necessarily guarantee her a rosy economic future. According to recent statistics:

• less than 9 percent of all females have incomes exceeding ten thousand dollars, compared to 45 percent of all males.

• the median income of a full-time female worker is 60 percent of the salary of her male counterpart.

• the female college graduate continues to earn less than a man with a high school education.

In light of these figures, it is obvious that the struggle for equal pay and equal opportunity must be a paramount consideration for women in the 1980s. However, the prospect of future change does not bring much immediate comfort to the divorced mother or the single woman struggling to make ends meet. Nor does it help the married woman whose independence is curtailed simply because her salary is so much lower than her husband's. What is the answer for these women, indeed, for our entire generation of women?

The first step must be the development of an entirely new attitude about money. We must educate ourselves, from scratch if need be, and realize how important money is to a woman, not because it can buy us status or a luxurious lifestyle but because it is the very foundation of our emotional security and a major route to freedom and happiness.

Whether we like it or not, in our world self-esteem and power are inextricably linked to earning capacity and money. The woman making twenty thousand dollars a year has an array of choices not available to her poorer sisters: She has the freedom to walk away from an unhappy marriage or an unsatisfying job; she has the security of knowing that she doesn't need to marry; she has the power to insist on an equal partnership in her marriage. In short, having money in the bank protects us against anxiety and frustrating dependence on others. If we lose our jobs, our husbands, or our health, at least we have some bulwark against the bill collectors who will come knocking at our doors. *Building a nest egg is as important as building a friendship or a support system.*

Many of the psychological problems women have are directly related to their feelings of financial powerlessness. Some single women, like my friend described above, often marry or enter relationships simply to escape what they perceive to be their precarious financial future. And married women suffer as well. Because most do not earn as much money as their husbands, they have less decision-making power in their relationships and generally bear the brunt of the domestic responsibilities. After all, their husbands reason, we're still the primary breadwinners; we can't fritter away our time on chores when we have important work to do. Since money translates into power, it's difficult for women to counteract this argument and assert themselves from a position of genuine equality.

Moreover, women can no longer count on marriage for

their financial security in the way they could in the past. And married women who want to divorce are often afraid or unable to do so, since they're so financially dependent on their husbands. In fact, when we consider the plight of the over-thirty divorced woman in our society, we can see that their fears are all too genuine.

The Divorce Crisis and Money

"Divorce brings an economic crisis for the majority of women," reports Brigham Young University sociologist Stan Albrecht. "Men don't have such a crisis. Men sometimes have an increase in income after divorce."

The University of Michigan's Institute for Social Research agrees. "The economic status of former husbands improves, while that of former wives deteriorates."

Women in this study confirmed these findings.

> *My husband left me for his secretary. He said I had become a child in the marriage because I stopped working to raise my children and didn't earn any money. After our divorce, he was never responsible about sending money for the children.*
>
> *I moved into the city with my kids and became an assistant buyer for basement dresses, earning one hundred dollars a week. The only way I could have earned more would have been to work in a fancier store, but that would have meant working Thursday night and Saturdays. I couldn't handle the guilt of being a working parent as it was. I still keep thinking the reason my daughter is fat is that I didn't have time to read to her at night.*
>
> *My husband now has his own business in California and a luxurious life-style. The bitterness I*

feel is that he didn't take care of the children when we desperately needed the money.

A thirty-five-year-old mother

Nine years ago I married an ambitious man in the music business. I became pregnant and left my job to raise the children. That was the beginning of the end of my self-confidence.

I won't say I gave up a booming career, but I subordinated whatever career drive and personal ambition I had to establish him and his business. Now that he's become successful, he says, "I don't need you anymore."

He left me now and I'm frightened. He won't pay alimony. I have to find a job and raise my children alone, too.

The thirty-two-year-old mother
of twins

While writing this chapter, I sat in on a divorce conference for a thirty-eight-year-old woman and her forty-year-old husband. They are Italian Catholics. Joe is a carpenter, earning twenty-two thousand dollars a year; Angie has been a homemaker all her life. They have three children, ages eleven through fourteen.

They were separating at Angie's instigation. She bitterly resented the fact that her father had not given her the college education he gave her brother. Instead, he had encouraged her to marry when she was only nineteen. In her midthirties, she had enrolled at a local community college and earned an associate's degree. She wanted the divorce because she and Joe no longer had anything in common. He hadn't bothered to improve himself the way she had, she told me. Furthermore, she wanted to go to work now that the children were older, but he felt that she should continue to stay home to cater to him and the children. He believed that he would become less of a man if she became independent.

At the meeting they arrived at the following monetary settlement: Joe agreed to give her their jointly owned home worth forty thousand dollars. Angie will, of course, have to meet the payments on the remaining twenty-thousand-dollar mortgage by herself. He will pay one hundred and twenty-five dollars a week in child support for his children. He will not pay alimony. She plans to work in the county office as a clerk and will earn between eight thousand and eleven thousand dollars a year.

This, I later learned, is a *typical* divorce settlement. Wife and children rarely receive more than one-third of the husband's income because the courts want him to have the incentive and the opportunity to remarry.

Later, I privately told this woman's lawyer that I thought his client's settlement was disastrous. How could she hope to meet the mortgage payments and feed the children on her small salary? Child support wouldn't even pay for dentist bills.

According to my figures, when we subtract the six thousand dollars child support the husband will pay, he will still be living, before taxes, on sixteen thousand dollars a year. Assuming his wife earns eight thousand dollars a year, she and her three children will live on fourteen thousand dollars a year. Sixteen thousand dollars for one man; fourteen thousand dollars for one woman and three children.

Furthermore, this woman will not only hold a full-time job but will have the major responsibility for raising their three children. The new burdens of a job and single parenthood certainly will not catapult Angie into the stereotypical "gay divorcée" life-style.

Who Is Getting Alimony?

When I asked her lawyer why women were not receiving much child support, let alone alimony, he replied: "When a woman wants out, she doesn't deserve anything from a man. A woman should not be awarded for leaving her husband. We of the law believe she is making a knowing and intelligent decision."

His opinion is echoed by most lawyers and judges. As one judge told a thirty-five-year-old divorcée in this study: "You girls asked for liberation. Now go out and be liberated. But don't expect your husbands to foot the bill."

In fact, it is the rare woman who is expecting her husband to foot the bill. Most women are more than willing to support themselves, but it is reasonable to expect former husbands to take some responsibility, especially when there are children involved.

- According to figures released in January 1979 in *Time* magazine, only 2 percent of all divorced women with children receive more than five thousand dollars a year in child support.
- According to figures released by the *New York Times,* only one-quarter of mothers who were divorced were receiving child support.
- In 1975 the average amount of money women were receiving in alimony was $2,430 a year.
- The poverty rate for women not receiving child support is 32 percent.
- Only 4 percent of the four and a half million women divorced or separated received alimony in 1975, according to the Survey of Income and Education undertaken by the federal government.

In light of these statistics, it is ironic that so many women believe that the Equal Rights Amendment will take away their alimony rights. The truth is those rights have already been lost.

The Displaced Homemaker

Penny was working as a secretary at the Museum of Modern Art in New York City when she met George, a banker. She was twenty-five when they married, and at his insistence she quit her job. He told her that he wanted to take care of her.

Over the years George became very successful. Penny took care of him and their son, as well as their luxurious city apartment and their weekend country home. She also entertained George's clients frequently.

The trouble started, Penny thinks, when she began the menopause at thirty-nine. "I had a difficult time. I had hot flashes. I was up in the middle of the night. I felt like I was going to throw up. I think George became repulsed and frightened. Maybe this made him realize we were both getting older."

A few months later George announced that he was moving into his own apartment in order to think about what he wanted from life. Shortly thereafter, Penny heard that he was spending weekends with a twenty-three-year-old career woman.

She was devastated by their separation. What had gone wrong? After years devoted to building a comfortable life-style for them, George now felt that Penny should be more "independent" and have her own career. Women who led their own lives, he told her, were more stimulating.

They saw a marriage counselor for a while, and then each went into private therapy. They "dated" sporadically while Penny waited for him to come back.

Because she was worried about money, she took a part-time job selling at Bonwit Teller's and another part-time position as a hatcheck girl in a nightclub.

Penny is a "displaced homemaker"—defined as any person who has been caring for family members and has lost economic support through divorce or death. Many women like Penny have not held a job for years; some have never worked outside the home. Consequently, a majority face a financially precarious and uncertain future.

The term *displaced homemaker* often conjures up the image of a woman who is old and gray, who has spent the last thirty years of her life wearing an apron. However, many displaced homemakers are mothers in their thirties with young children to support.

A social worker with the Jewish Family Service told me, "It's terribly hard for women today. Let's say a woman's husband walked out ten years ago, and she still had children at home. Just the fact that she was alone raising her children would have been considered brave and courageous. She would have received a lot of sympathy and esteem.

"However, today, she's not only supposed to raise her children alone but to become a corporate president as well. Become a corporate president! It's hard for her to even get out of bed in the morning, she's so depressed. It's even hard for her to have sympathy for herself. In her mind, she believes she's done everything wrong."

No-Fault Divorce Laws

Although the women's liberation movement has often been blamed for the woes of the divorced woman, in fact the first no-fault divorce laws in this country were passed in California early in 1969 by a male legislature. Under no-fault divorce statutes, it is not necessary to prove any of the traditional grounds, like adultery or mental cruelty, in order to win a divorce.

As Riane Eisler says in the *Equal Rights Handbook,* "The feminist movement is seeing a resurgence in this country, not as the cause but as a result of the dislocations American women are undergoing today."

Divorced women are suffering not because of the women's movement but because their lives are still in the hands of male judges and lawyers who decide on the kinds of settlements they will receive. To date, forty-seven state legislatures—staffed by male politicians—have adopted no-fault divorce laws.

This has hurt many women badly.

> *My husband left me and remarried a year later to a gal seventeen years younger, whom he was seeing all along. It's been about a year and a half since the divorce. I'm angry, frustrated, disappointed, and lonely. It's a rough row to hoe by yourself. I have negative feelings toward men, although I still want someone to take care of me and need me.*
>
> *Before my divorce I was self-assured, and almost egotistical in my security. I followed my husband around for nineteen years of military benefits. No-fault divorce is for the birds! Women devote their lives to men, and for what? Not to get one red cent or even thanks!*
>
> A thirty-nine-year-old
> computer operator for the
> U.S. Navy in Florida

The "no alimony" syndrome fails to recognize a woman's real economic contribution to the household—the cooking, cleaning, nurturing, and sex that a bachelor would have to pay for. A woman is never reimbursed for her wifing career. Where are her retirement benefits? Her pension plan? Her severance allowance? Her unemployment insurance?

In many cases, the over-thirty woman is expected to launch a career overnight and raise her children, too. We are not allowed the luxury of establishing our careers while someone else takes care of us and raises our children. How many men would have been able to make it in the business world without the support and backup from their wives?

Moreover, those who argue against alimony forget that a homemaker's earning capacity has been eroded during her marriage. If she has to return to work, she will start at entry-level pay, while her husband can continue to earn a salary built up over the years.

The National Organization for Women has studied the problems of the divorced woman and calls for the following changes:

• When a noncustodial spouse leaves the state, the original support order will retain jurisdiction. This would prevent men from moving out-of-state to avoid paying child support.

• Wage garnishment should be done automatically, as this seems to be the most effective way of ensuring prompt and sufficient payments. Without garnishment, many men don't pay.

• All departments of the federal government shall cooperate to the fullest with states trying to locate non-supporting or out-of-state parents.

• Uniform national levels of support shall be promoted, based on governmental cost of living indices.

• The word *alimony* shall be changed to *entitlement*. Entitlement may be awarded to a dependent spouse or one who cannot make as much as one-half of her husband's income. When the marriage is of less than twenty years duration, entitlement shall be awarded for however many years the marriage lasted.

• Grievance procedures against attorneys and judges shall be strengthened.

These reforms are of crucial importance to provide divorced women with the financial security they so desperately need.

The Independent Divorcée

Divorce does not have to precipitate economic crisis. A woman who is economically independent may suffer emotional trauma in the aftermath of divorce, but she will not face the economic anxieties common to so many displaced homemakers. Money can become the crucial difference between nightmare and freedom, as the following story attests.

Laura was raised in a Catholic convent. She married at nineteen and had two children in quick succession. "I used to love to dress up the kids, go to the supermarket, and show off. Everybody would say to me, 'Oh, you look too young to be their mother.' "

In her late twenties she became restless and had an affair with a man she met in a local theater group. "I felt very guilty, but I continued with the affair because it was my first experience with oral sex, and I didn't want it to end."

She had never responded to her husband in the same way and the marriage soon ended.

She lived alone for four years, until she was thirty-one. "I was poor and lived in an inner-city ghetto with my kids. I took a job as a receptionist in a furniture showroom."

To her surprise, her ability to deal with people was so exceptional that she became the showroom manager. Shortly thereafter, she met a divorced man with one son who became her second husband.

A year after their marriage, they founded a furniture business together. Their income zoomed to over one hundred and twenty-five thousand dollars a year. "I had no idea I was such a good businesswoman," she said. "However, what I learned about myself is that my energy won't quit."

However, when she and I talked, she said that the marriage was not as successful as their business partnership. "We go through long periods of aggravation with each other," she told me. "On the weekends I feel like a police officer with the children, and he won't back me up. The TV blares, while I'd like to listen to some peaceful music. I love my kids, but I often have fantasies of escaping from them."

I left Laura that day and tucked away her story in my folder. A year later, on a hunch, I wrote to ask what had happened to her marriage. I suspected it was on the rocks. Her return letter confirmed my feelings: "I am divorced now, living alone in an apartment while the contractors work on the town house I've just purchased.

"My husband and I parted in June by mutual consent. My daughter (she's nineteen) has already moved into an apartment on her own. The two boys (eighteen and fifteen) chose to stay with their father in order to be near their school and friends. I must admit I am delighted to be cut loose from all my former obligations. Actually, motherhood is very deceiving because people always expect a mother to never stop mothering, while the children get so tired of being mothered!

"I'm dating a handsome architect, and we're going to Jamaica in two weeks.

"I kept the corporation and the stocks, and my ex-husband took the house. I pay him three hundred dollars a month in child support. The business is going strong, and I love not having to consider another opinion both in my personal and business life. It's not that I'm not interested in anyone else's view; it's just that for once I'm not forced to act on another's whim. I'll never marry again."

* * *

With money in our pockets, we women can do anything we want to do, be anyone we want to be. Our potential is limitless.

But, first, women have to reeducate themselves about money, and to this end I offer some of the suggestions sent in by Laura and other women who have achieved genuine financial independence.

• Read books about money. Learn to develop a positive attitude and overcome any lingering remnants of math anxiety. Think of managing money as a pleasurable activity —a way of testing your intelligence. Take courses; start or join study groups and investment clubs with other men and women.

• If at all possible, buy property, and in other ways tax shelter your money. I heard from women who had invested in cows, stocks, certificates of deposit compounded daily, or Treasury bonds. Some went on to buy businesses or even shopping centers.

• Find trusted advisers—an accountant, a stockbroker, an insurance salesperson, a banker and (in higher income brackets) a tax lawyer. Successful women do not rely only on themselves but bond with others and form teams so that they can make their money work for them.

• Negotiate suitable raises and bonuses, and if they are available, get involved in your company's pension and profit-sharing plans. Bank or invest a portion of each paycheck.

• Devise a workable budget and stick to it. Curb impulsive spending. However, *do* set aside money for yourself. Invest wisely in a wardrobe that expresses the image you want to project at work. Pamper yourself, at times, with massages, relaxing vacations, and self-improvement courses. Pleasure is a necessary part of life.

• If you are married and dependent on your husband's income, make sure that some property (including stocks and bonds) as well as charge accounts are in your name only.

For today's woman Virginia Woolf's vision of a "room of one's own" is not enough. She must strive for a house of her own, property of her own. Only by establishing solid roots can a woman overcome anxiety and build a base of financial security. Once women achieve the same salaries, benefits, and privileges that men have taken for granted, they will find that they feel less like "good girls" and more like powerful women, women whose egos reflect their bulging bank accounts.

9

On To Our Forties and Beyond

I remember, as a teenager, listening to my grandmother and her friends clucking to one another, their gray heads shaking, their mouths twitching with repressed pain. How times flies, they used to say. How time flies.

I was secretly impatient with them. Like all young fools, I believed I would be young forever, that getting older would never happen to me. But my grandmother was right, the years do fly by. Before we know it, we'll be forty, forty-five, fifty. But women who have lived fully and struggled to make their dreams come true can accept the years as they come without fear. Listen to these words of wisdom from one of the women I talked to, a fifty-three-year-old successful attorney and mother of three.

> *I got divorced when I was thirty-six, and the first two years were absolute hell. I hadn't worked since I quit my secretarial job at twenty-four to get married, and suddenly I had to support myself and my children. I was terrified of the future. I had visions*

of myself at seventy, a lonely, little old lady, bitter
about the turns my life had taken. But eventually
I pulled myself together, and I went to law school
when I was thirty-seven.

   Now, I have no fears about aging. I know that
when I'm seventy or seventy-five, I can look back
and say, 'God, how I've lived. How I've enjoyed.
How I've laughed. How great it all was.'

   I've come to believe that anyone who pursues
their dreams won't regret the past or fear the future.
But those who are too timid, too frightened to take
risks, how bitter they will feel. How sad and angry.
How betrayed. How furious with themselves. All
of us are given only one life, and it's up to us, and
no one else, to make something of that life—some-
thing meaningful to us.

Our generation of women is extremely fortunate because we have a choice, we can, unlike our mothers and
grandmothers, re-create our lives—ourselves—in our thirties,
forties, and fifties if we wish. We have the freedom to walk
away from an unhappy marriage; we can decide whether or
not we want to be a parent; we can become anything we
want to become. Today's generation of women won't have
to sit around when they're seventy and bemoan their wasted
lives.

   In order to enjoy our maturity, we must break free
from our "good girl" training and become assertive, independent, and pleasure-loving. We cannot approach our mature years with ghosts from the past. A friend's mother once
told her, "Women should be shot after forty." And, indeed,
there was a time when a woman had no options after forty,
when menopause brought an end to her possibilities. Once
a woman's early beauty and ability to bear children was
finished, she was finished. Only youth had any meaning for

women who lived within the feminine mystique. Anatomy was destiny.

However, we live in an exciting new time for women. One only has to look at women like Jane Fonda, Gloria Steinem, Sophia Loren, and Marlo Thomas to see how glamorous and sexy over-forty women can be. These women have a worldly charm, a patina of *savoir-faire,* that younger women simply do not have. Sophistication and depth are by-products of experience.

As one woman wrote, "When I was thirty, I had a friend who was forty. I called her and asked her what it would be like to be forty. She said, 'When you turned thirty, did you wish that you were twenty?' I said no, that would be like saying I wish I hadn't lived. She said, 'Well, it doesn't change, it just goes on.' I found this exhilarating."

Women who live their lives fully speak of the richness of maturity.

> *Life began at forty! I divorced my husband, and the shackles were gone. I met a man thirteen years younger than me and for the first time visited Alaska and Niagara Falls. I've never had so much fun.*
>
> A forty-one-year-old woman
> from Kansas City

> *The revelations that come to a mature mind can be incredible.*
>
> A forty-three-year-old poet

> *The forties are a wonderful age for a woman. You know what life is all about by then.*
>
> A forty-two-year-old business-
> woman

Women today are saying no to traditional definitions of womanhood. We are proclaiming the right not just to find ourselves but to create ourselves, to *develop* our own identities. For us the future is promising and bright. For women today it is never too late. We have nothing to lose as we make new choices and everything to gain.

Moreover, the youth culture is on the wane. In 1970 the median age of the average American was just under twenty-eight. Today, in 1980, the median age is thirty-five. By the year 2030 when thirty-five-year-old women will be eighty-five, one person in five will be over sixty-five.

The 1980s must be a decade of social change. Men and women should learn that real comradeship is possible within marriage. This not only will free women from domestic oppression but will set the stage for a new way of relating between the sexes which, in turn, will affect attitudes in the workplace. Once men view women as equal in privilege, men will not as readily shut women out from the halls of status and power. If we can't win equal rights in our own marriages, how will we ever win equal rights in the culture at large? We owe it, not only to ourselves and our men but to our sons and our daughters to create a model of a truly equal partnership between men and women. We women, the mothers of the future generations, have the power to raise our children in role-free, nonsexist ways.

As part of our struggle for equality with men, we must work to set up education centers as adjuncts to our schools. Barbara M. Wertheimer, the author of *We Were There: The Story of Working Women in America,* tells us that there are six million children of child-care age, and only one million available places in reliable centers today. And Elizabeth Roden, professor and chairperson of the English and Communication Department at Golden Gate University, sees lack of child-care facilities as one of the major barriers facing women.

Critics of child care charge that it will lead to a breakdown of the American family. But that is not true. The point is that new mores have evolved, and, as a result, our society has more single parents than ever before in its history. More married women work. Child care, or education, centers would simply help to ease the burdens wrought by these new changes so that women could enjoy family life more. America must evolve new social structures in our increasingly complicated world.

Whether or not these changes occur depends, in large part, on whether women, in the next two years, win the battle for the Equal Rights Amendment.

The need for a federal ERA has been proven by women's experiences in the state of Pennsylvania, which was one of the first states to adopt a state ERA in 1971. On the basis of their ERA:

• The state sued the Pennsylvania Interscholastic Athletic Association and won for female high school students the right to go out for interscholastic sports.

• A woman may not be fired if she becomes pregnant.

• Insurance policies must offer equal benefits to men and women in the same age and health categories.

• Medical and disability insurance must cover the complications of pregnancy.

• Girls do not have to wait until they are eighteen to get newspaper routes. They can carry papers at twelve, as boys have always done.

The ERA in Pennsylvania has *not* integrated toilet facilities (although on airplanes, they have always been integrated) ; nor have women been called up for the draft. The attorney general has stated that the right to separate toilet facilities is protected by the constitutional right of privacy. Moreover, protective labor laws for women have not been repealed.

Winning the ERA is crucial for all women. If we don't

succeed on this issue, men will see us as impotent losers who cannot get Constitutional backing for entitlement. Without ERA, women will continue to make approximately half of what men make, and affirmative action programs will be threatened as well. It will be much more difficult for a woman to sue in a discrimination case and win.

The backlash against women's rights is already evident as a result of our failure to ratify the ERA. Sears Roebuck and Co., for example, one of the nation's largest employers, has just filed suit against ten federal agencies, including the Justice Department, Equal Opportunities Employment Commission (EEOC) and the Bureau of the Census, charging that their actions and inactions have created a predominantly white male work force. Sears argues that since the government has failed to abolish discrimination in its own house and has failed to enforce civil rights and equal opportunity laws effectively, private employers such as Sears should not be forced to comply with those laws! More and more, we will see private companies trying to subvert the push for equal opportunity.

Without ERA, moreover, we will not have the clout to demand that corporations institute management training programs for over-thirty women. We will continue to feel powerless and continue to be forced to accept low-status, dead-end jobs. We will not have the money to provide ourselves and our children with the necessities and luxuries of life.

To win our victories, we must bond together in sisterhood. We must organize. Women must stop fighting with one another—corporate executive vs. secretary, homemaker vs. career woman, young woman vs. older woman.

"Sisterhood is dead," a woman I had known for ten years told me recently. We had met when the feminist movement was still in its infancy, and we emerged from consciousness raising to proclaim our love and support for each other. During those early, heady days, the CR group I belonged to wrote a book together and donated the money we made to the fight for ERA. We agonized over the rape of the women of Bangladesh and put our energies into running women's centers and counseling rape victims. I believed with all my heart that we were in the process of creating a brave new world.

However, this woman now tells me that her spirit, and that of many women she knows, has vanished. "The communal love of the sixties and seventies is gone," she says. "Today, it's dog eat dog. If there are ten women in a corporation, only two will make partner. With that kind of competition, how can there be sisterhood?"

A twenty-one-year-old woman who just graduated from college was amazed when I told her that her generation needed to bond with older generations. "Your generation did all the work," she said. "There aren't any issues for us to take up anymore. Why does there have to be sisterhood?" There has to be sisterhood, I answer, because there are still many pressing social issues to be solved. The rise in crime, for example, is an issue around which all women can unite. The rape rate has risen dramatically, and many women, especially in big cities, are afraid to be on the streets after dark.

We also see that child-care payments to divorced women are not being enforced by the courts and that wife batterers are not being prosecuted. These three instances show us how the criminal justice system has broken down in America, adversely affecting women's lives.

One of my hopes is that we will assume our rightful place in the political world as we make the transition from compliant "good girls" to mature, responsible women.

Although women won the right to vote fifty years ago, we have never shown our political muscle. How many women are articulate about political issues? How many women read the newspapers from cover to cover the way men do?

The apolitical woman is the woman who can't break out of the "good girl" role. Submissive and passive, she accepts the fact that women are no longer awarded alimony, that pornography demeans her, that the government is not providing her with day-care centers, although she pays taxes.

The mature woman, however, feels entitled to have her needs met by her society, and she asserts her voice with all her passion and dignity.

A good example of the mature, self-actualizing woman is Eleanor Roosevelt, who can be a role model to us because she too only found her strength, her power, her voice, on the other side of thirty. When she was in her twenties, she subordinated herself to her husband and his mother and, as a result, was often depressed, deep in what she would call her Griselda moods.

She turned thirty as World War I broke out, a tragedy which, ironically, gave her the freedom to plunge into community life. Her first activity at thirty-five was taking charge of the Red Cross Recreation Room at the U.S. Naval Hospital.

From there, she went back to school to learn typing and shorthand. At thirty-six she began to do some public speaking for the first time in her life—something that would have terrified her when she was younger. It was that year too that she became interested in politics and went along on the campaign trail when her husband was nominated for vice-president. Soon she became a political personality in her own right.

American women have long thought of themselves as more progressive and independent than women in other parts of the world. However, both India and Great Britain now have women leaders; we do not. Where is the American

Indira Gandhi? Margaret Thatcher? Golda Meir? Where are our female senators? Our congresspeople?

Women in America remain outside the real centers of power. According to a report released by the Center for American Women and Politics at the Eagleton Institute at Rutgers University, thousands of women are beginning to run for local office. Most, however, are running for low-paying or unsalaried jobs.

At the same time there has been a decline in the number of women in Congress and a decline in women federal judges.

Recent figures show women—who make up 51 percent of the population—hold only 9 percent of the seats in their state legislatures and 11 percent of state cabinet and executive offices. Only 3 percent are county commissioners, and 8 percent are mayors. Of six hundred and seventy-five circuit and district court judges, only five were women.

With percentages like these, how can women expect to win divorce rights or equal pay? Power won't be handed to us; we'll have to move in and take it.

As this study has shown, women become more ambitious, more assertive, sexier, mentally healthier, and more confident on the other side of thirty. We are breaking all the rules, and old timetables do not apply. For us anything is possible. It is not too late because new, exciting beginnings happen every day on the other side of thirty.

Chapter Notes

Chapter 1

p. 17. These statistics were gleaned from *Passages* by Gail Sheehy, and from the results of this study.

Chapter 2

p. 25. This data comes from the work of G. Gurin, *Americans View Their Mental Health*, New York: Basic Books, 1960. Also from G. Knupfer, "The Mental Health of the Unmarried," *American Journal of Psychiatry*, 122:841–851, 1966.

p. 27. This story appeared in the *Ladies' Home Journal*, January, 1955.

p. 31. Information supplied by the National Organization for Women.

Chapter 3

p. 45. Ann Landers devoted three columns to this finding: November 3, 1975; March 29, 1976; and January 23, 1976.

p. 65. See Bibliography for a listing of some of Abraham Maslow's books.

Chapter 4

p. 69. "Attitudes of Unmarried Men and Women," a dissertation presented to the Graduate Faculty of the School of Human Behavior, United States International University, by Nancy Archibald Douglas, Ph.D., 1977.

p. 71. From "The Population Factor and Urban Structure," by William Alonso, Center for Population Studies, Harvard University (Working Paper number 102, August, 1977). Also from "Social Policy and the Life Cycle: A Developmental Perspective," by Larry Hirschorn, University of Pennsylvania, printed in the *Social Service Review*, September, 1977.

p. 86. From the Nancy Archibald Douglas dissertation, "Attitudes of Unmarried Men and Women."

Chapter 7

p. 162. "U.S. Working Women: A Data Book," U.S. Department of Labor, *Bureau of Labor Statistics Bulletin*.

p. 167. From *The Decade of Women: A Ms. History of the 70s in Words and Pictures.* A *Ms.* book, edited by the *Ms.* magazine staff and published by Putnam.

p. 171. Quote from *Business Week* article on "Corporate Women," appearing in the November 24, 1975 issue.

p. 173. The Johnson O'Connor Research Institute (11 E. 62nd Street, New York City) published two studies: "Women Born to Manage," by Michael L. Johnson, first printed in *Industry Week*, August 4, 1975, and "The Potential of Women," by John Durkin, published by the Institute.

Chapter 8

p. 195. From the National Organization for Women.

p. 200. From *The New York Times,* July 2, 1979.

p. 204. From the National Organization for Women.

Chapter 9

p. 217. Courtesy of the Women's Political Caucus.

A Selected Bibliography

Bardwick, Judith. *Psychology of Women: A Study of Bio-cultural Conflicts.* New York: Harper & Row, 1971.

Bell, Alan, and Martin Weinberg. *Homosexualities: A Study of Diversity Among Men and Women.* New York: Simon & Schuster, 1978.

Bird, Caroline. *The Two-Paycheck Marriage.* New York: Rawson, Wade, 1979.

Bolles, Richard Nelson. *What Color Is Your Parachute? A Practical Manual for Career Changers.* Berkeley, CA: Ten Speed Press, 1979.

Chesler, Phyllis. *Women and Madness.* New York: Avon, 1972.

Davis, Elizabeth Gould. *The First Sex.* New York: Penguin Books, 1972.

De Beauvoir, Simone. *The Second Sex.* New York: Vintage, 1974.

De Rosis, Helen, and Victoria Pellegrino. *The Book of Hope: How Women Overcome Depression.* New York: Bantam Books, 1976.

Dible, Donald. *Up Your Own Organization: A Handbook on How to Start and Finance a New Business.* Vacaville, CA: The Entrepreneur Press, 1974.

Douglas, Nancy Archibald. "Attitudes of Unmarried Men and Women." Ph.D. dissertation presented to the Graduate Faculty of the School of Human Behavior, United States International University, 1977.

Edwards, Marie, and Eleanor Hoover. *The Challenge of Being Single.* New York: New American Library, 1975.

Eisler, Riane. *The Equal Rights Handbook.* New York: Avon, 1978.

Farley, Lin. *Sexual Shakedown: The Sexual Harassment of Women on the Job.* New York: McGraw-Hill, 1978.

Friday, Nancy. *My Mother, My Self: The Daughter's Search for Identity.* New York: Dell, 1978.

Friedan, Betty. *The Feminine Mystique.* New York: Dell, 1963.

Gould, Roger. *Transformations.* New York: Simon & Schuster, 1978.

Granzig, William, and Ellen Peck. *The Parent Test: How to Measure and Develop Your Talent for Parenthood.* New York: G. P. Putnam's Sons, 1978.

Hirschorn, Larry. "Social Policy and the Life Cycle: A Developmental Perspective." *Social Service Review* (September, 1977).

Hite, Shere. *The Hite Report.* New York: Macmillan, 1976.

Horney, Karen. *Neurosis and Human Growth.* New York: W. W. Norton, 1950.

Howe, Louis. *Pink Collar Workers: Inside the World of Women's Work.* New York: G. P. Putnam's Sons, 1977.

Levinson, Daniel. *The Seasons of a Man's Life.* New York: Knopf, 1978.

Maslow, Abraham. *Dominance, Self-Esteem and Self-Actualization.* Monterey, CA: Brooks, Cole, 1973.

————. *Farther Reaches of Human Nature.* New York: Penguin Books, 1976.

————. *New Pathways in Psychology.* New York: Taplinger, 1972.

Masters, William, and Virginia Johnson. *Homosexuality in Perspective.* Boston: Little, Brown, 1979.

Montagu, Ashley. *The Natural Superiority of Women.* New York: Macmillan, 1977.

Napolitane, Catherine, and Victoria Pellegrino. *Living and Loving After Divorce.* New York: New American Library, 1978.

Ponse, Barbara. *Identities in the Lesbian World.* Westport, CT: Greenwood, 1978.

Porter, Sylvia. *Sylvia Porter's Money Book.* New York: Avon, 1976.

Price, Jane. *You're Not Too Old to Have a Baby.* New York: Penguin Books, 1978.

Robinson, Marie. *Power of Sexual Surrender.* New York: New American Library.

Roesch, Roberta. *There's Always a Right Job for Every Woman.* New York: Berkley Books, 1978.

Schlayer, Mary Elizabeth, and Marilyn H. Cooley. *How to Be a Financially Secure Woman*. New York: Rawson, Wade, 1978.

Sheehy, Gail. *Passages: Predictable Crises of Adult Life*. New York: E. P. Dutton, 1976.

Walker, Lenore. *The Battered Woman*. New York: Harper & Row, 1979.

Wertheimer, Barbara. *We Were There: The Story of Working Women in America*. New York: Pantheon, 1977.

Appendix
Sample Thirties Questionnaire

Age _____ City and State _____
Single, married, divorced or widowed _____
Number of children _____ Their ages _____
Employment _____
Race or religion _____

PART I

1. The facts of your life may have changed considerably since you entered your thirties. Perhaps you left home, left your husband, changed jobs, changed fields, went back to school, had a baby, bought a house, entered therapy, lost fifty pounds or took up tennis. Please specify the two or three most important events that occurred at each age, and the predominant feelings you had during that year. Anger? Frustration? Exhilaration? Fright? Confusion? Loneliness? Boredom? Satisfaction? Sadness? Confidence? Desperation? Inertia?

30 _____
31 _____

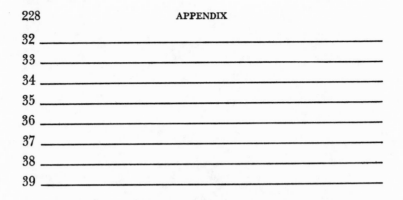

32 _____

33 _____

34 _____

35 _____

36 _____

37 _____

38 _____

39 _____

PART II: QUESTIONS FOR MARRIED WOMEN

2. How long have you been married? _____

_____

3. Do you and your husband share more or less than you did when you were first married? _____

_____

4. What are the pressures in your marriage? _____

_____

5. Describe any extramarital affairs you've had in your thirties _____

_____

6. Do you and your husband agree on whether you want children? _____

_____

7. How is your marriage different from what you expected it to be? _____

_____

8. Can you see yourself married to your husband for the rest of your life? _____

_____

PART II: QUESTIONS FOR FORMERLY MARRIED WOMEN

2. How long have you been single and how does it make you feel?_____

_____

3. How much care do you put into decorating and maintaining your home? _____

_____

4. Why aren't you married any longer? _____

_____

5. Are you seeing one man (or woman) regularly, several simultaneously, one after another, next to no one, or no one at all? _____

_____

6. How has your approach to men changed? _____

_____

7. If you aren't a mother, would you consider having children while you're single? _____

_____

8. If you have children, how do you feel about being a single mother? _____

_____

PART II: QUESTIONS FOR SINGLE WOMEN

2. How much care do you put into decorating and maintaining your home? _____

_____

3. Are you seeing one man (or woman) regularly, several simultaneously, one after another, next to no one, or no one at all? _____

_____

4. What do you look for in a lover? _____

5. Are these the same qualities you sought in your twenties?

6. Do you feel differently about being single in your thirties from the way you did in your twenties (likes and dislikes) ? _____

7. How have your love relationships changed since you turned thirty? _____

8. Would you consider having children while you're single?

PART III: QUESTIONS FOR EVERYONE

9. Step by step, how did you get where you are in your career? _____

10. How does what you're doing differ from the expectations you had in your twenties? _____

11. Have you found a mentor or have you become one?

12. What can you see yourself doing five years from now?

13. How have your feelings about having children changed since your twenties? _____

_____

14. If you have children, how has motherhood changed you in your thirties? _____

_____

15. How have your friendships changed since you turned thirty? _____

16. How has your relationship with your parents changed since you turned thirty? _____

_____

17. What things in your life do you want to change? _____

_____

18. What situations make you feel inadequate? _____

_____

19. Do you feel differently about your body now from the way you did in your twenties? _____

_____

20. Do you enjoy sex more or less than you did in your twenties? _____

_____

21. In what ways do you see yourself differently from the way you did in your thirties? _____

_____

22. How has your approach to life changed since you turned thirty? _____

_____

23. Please use this space for anything else that's on your mind. And thank you! _____

_____

Index